ARCHIE MACPHERSON was born and raised in Shettleston in the east-end of Glasgow. He was headteacher of Swinton School, Lanarkshire, before he began his broadcasting career at the BBC in 1962. It was here that he became the principal commentator and presenter on Sportscene. He has since worked with STV, Eurosport, Talksport, Radio Clyde and Setanta. He has commentated on various key sporting events including three Olympic Games and six FIFA World Cups. In 2005 he received a Scottish BAFTA for special contribution to Scottish broadcasting and was inducted into Scottish football's Hall of Fame in 2017.

By the same author:

Touching the Heights: Personal Portraits of Scottish Sporting Greats, Luath Press, 2022
More Than A Game: Living with the Old Firm 2020 Luath Press
Adventures in the Golden Age: Scotland in the World Cup Finals 1974–1998,
   Black and White Publishing, 2018
Silent Thunder, Ringwood Publishing, 2014
Jock Stein: The Definitive Biography, Racing Post Books, 2014
Undefeated: The Life and Times of Jimmy Johnstone, Celtic FC, 2010
A Game of Two Halves: The Autobiography, Black and White Publishing, 2009
Flower of Scotland?: A Scottish Football Odyssey, Highdown, 2005
Action Replays, Chapmans Publishers, 1991
The Great Derbies: Blue and Green, Rangers Versus Celtic, BBC Books, 1989

It's a Goal!

ARCHIE MACPHERSON

Luath Press Limited
EDINBURGH
www.luath.co.uk

First published 2024

ISBN: 978-1-804251-39-3

The author's right to be identified as author of this book
under the Copyright, Designs and Patents Act 1988
has been asserted.

This book is made of materials from well-managed,
FSC®-certified forests and other controlled sources.

Printed and bound by
Ashford Colour Press, Gosport

Typeset in 11.5 point Sabon by
Main Point Books, Edinburgh

© Archie Macpherson 2024

Dedicated to Pat Woods

Contents

Introduction   11

1. The First Hurrah   13
2. Local Hero   15
3. Tribalism   17
4. Starstruck   20
5. Pars for the Course   23
6. Auditioning   25
7. In at the Death   27
8. Nobody Does It Better   29
9. A Winning Head   32
10. End of an Era   34
11. Decimal Points   36
12. An Italian Dessert   38
13. Camera Chaos   42
14. A Foreign Foot   45
15. The Narrow Margin   48
16. The Breakthrough   50
17. World Beaters   53
18. Guid Gear   56
19. The Peak   58
20. Granite Approach   62
21. Full House   65
22. The Miscalculation   68

23.	Teenage Debut	71
24.	How to Burst a Coupon	74
25.	One Crowded Spanish Evening	77
26.	Studs to the Fore	81
27.	Arthur's Warning	84
28.	Drawing a Line	86
29.	Sassenach Intervention	89
30.	The First Hiccup	91
31.	The Odd Couple	93
32.	Raising the Temperature	95
33.	A New Kind of Pain	97
34.	Breaking the Mould	100
35.	The Finest Touch	103
36.	A Political Stew	105
37.	Delusion	107
38.	Hanging by a Thread	109
39.	Breakdown	113
40.	The Immortal Touch	115
41.	Stunning Finale	117
42.	Sipping Success	121
43.	Crowded Out	125
44.	A Likely Lad	130
45.	The Tartan Rebirth	134
46.	That Memorable Hug	138
47.	Withering Words	141
48.	The Saddest Night	145
49.	Heartache	149

50.	The Crumb of Comfort	154
51.	The English Accent	159
52.	The Pyrrhic Victory	164
53.	Topsy Turvy	168
54.	A Sending Off	173
55.	Mishap	177
56.	Sayonara Spectacle	182
57.	The End of the Affair	186

Acknowledgements   191

Introduction

GOALS SEEMED TO choreograph my life. Charged with the duty of commentating on football matches for nearly half a century, they seemed to route me through the passage of time. The significant ones stand erect like landmarks without which I could not look back on life with as much sense of order and the appreciation of one age merging into another. These included startling expulsions of my breath in World and European Cups as well as domestic football back to the days when I would stand and watch junior football as a boy readily infatuated with this marvellous sport on my doorstep. Not all the goals that lodged in the mind, never to be cast asunder, were spectacular. And some may even think my selection eccentric given that it is a very personal reflection of how I was affected by specific goals that may not have raised an eyebrow for others. They are MY goals, lodged within me for one reason or the other, lending a particular interpretation to a game that would particularly separate it from others. They also revive my recollections of the personality clashes and the political infighting that characterised so much of my time in this business. So, in every reminiscence there is a goal and scorer whom I list singly, and who makes me appreciate how privileged I was, not only to be a witness to these events but as a voice harmonising with them to perpetuate their significance.

Of course, I had the utmost admiration for the creative geniuses of football without whom goals would never have been scored. But a goalless game, whatever elegance and skill might have abounded throughout, I treated like a tasteless meal lacking these imperative condiments of flavour that separated victor from vanquished. I was also fortunate to have worked throughout a period which saw me experience six World Cups and was present when three Scottish clubs returned to these shores with European trophies. In all of this time I experienced different emotions recording these goals. They ranged from exultation, taking me from a seated position into an occasional leap of triumph that came with the automatic appreciation of excellence. Then there were the others that burdened you with obvious disappointment but which had to be pronounced like you were devoid of partiality. Of course, I was accused of bias from time to time but accepted that as an inevitable part of speaking into a microphone to a sensitive Scottish public which often pulled no punches as adjudicators of football broadcasters. They were skilled at that.

So the goals that clung on to me are here to be read as evidence of a man lucky enough to have had pre-broadcasting memories that indicated how stirred I was by goal-scoring from well before puberty. It was embedded in my nature as I try to show initially here. And of how, eventually, a microphone turned into a magnet that attracted irreplaceable memories of certain balls nestling in nets that also uncannily reflected the ups and downs of an unpredictable football life.

I

The First Hurrah

Scotland v England
13 April 1946
1–0
Goal: Jimmy Delaney

TO ACKNOWLEDGE THE ending of the Second World War and the return to what might pass as normality, my father took me to a football match. Many others had the same idea. Indeed, I always look back with pride that I helped create a statistic that stands out like a testament to survival after the ravages that the Luftwaffe heaped upon my part of the world. For 138,468 were inside Hampden Park on that special day, 13 April 1946. The Scotland–England game had been advertised as a Victory International that proposed a sense of collective celebration and a unity that had brought us through the war together. Except as I climbed up the steep stairs of the east end of Hampden I could sense the tribal anticipation amongst the Scots of wishing to deprive the English of the mantle of invincibility that had been worn since they had defeated us in the last match before the war, 15 April 1939, 2–1 at this very stadium. And hadn't they trounced us 6–1 in an 'unofficial' game in 1945 when we could hardly put a team together? This was the Auld Enemy no less. The bonding uniforms were out. Civvies were in.

So I was to view the Auld Enemy for the first time from a posture that was far from comfortable. I was wee. Everybody else was big. Then there was the squeeze half-way up that vast east terracing slope which was like being put alongside Hogmanay revellers in the last tram to Auchenshuggle. But help was on hand. In those days, small kids like me, would be passed over the heads of the crowds like 'pass-the-parcel', to comparative safety nearer the front, to the cries of, 'Watch the wean!' So, unknown to my mother I parted company with my father as I was transported over the heads of the crowd to just behind the perimeter wall from where I was to see a goal that lives with me to this day.

The players seemed gigantic to me down there, the English particularly so. They seemed like rough hooligans, bullying sergeant-majors, uncouth. Ours were cavaliers fighting a just cause. The blonde-haired Bobby Brown in the Scotland goal seem to exemplify for me the purity of their make-up as he gracefully pulled crosses out of the air despite the constant aggravation of the great England striker Tommy Lawton, the man they were to call 'The Hammer of the Scots', backed up as he was by talented midfield players Denis Compton and Len Shackleton. But the core of the Scottish defence, the two Shaw brothers and Frank Brennan at centre-half, all of whom came from the one small mining village in Lanarkshire, Annathill, never flinched.

Peering from the low position with no conception of time passing in the match but feeling growing frustration, the world suddenly exploded. There had only been two minutes of the game left in fact. Two great wingers who could cause an argument in an empty house about who was the superior, Willie Waddell of Rangers and Jimmy Delaney of Celtic, combined to convert 139,468 into a seething cauldron.

Jackie Husband takes a free kick. Waddell gets his head to a ball in the air, deflecting it into the path of Delaney who crashes it (as I can recollect) into the net. The game has been won, snatched from the deadening clutches of a no-scoring draw. In the madness around me I experience a personal feeling that I still think ranks with any sensuality I was ever to feel in adult life. But, from that moment, in a sense I never did grow up.

For that small Hampden boy was with me every time I raised a mike to my mouth with the Auld Enemy in sight. He was inside me, kicking every ball for Scotland as I tried to retain professional objectivity, although both of us nakedly desperate to relive another tumultuous Delaney moment.

2

Local Hero

Shettleston Juniors v Vale of Clyde
Late 1940s
Cup game (but which tournament I can't really recall although being a kind of local derby it felt of global significance)
Goal: 'Doc' McManus

THE FIRST STOP after getting out of the cradle was Shettleston Juniors or the 'Town' as they were called. Now ludicrously renamed Glasgow United FC, thus deprived of its special identity. They wore the white shirts of neutrality in an area that was self-consciously sectarian and because of which much time was devoted to determining which foot you kicked with. 'Doc' McManus united both persuasions because he seemed to represent the honest endeavour of those men in dungarees who would come straight from their work on a Saturday, visit the bookie, have a snort in the pub and then to the game, bawling threats to certain players that they would have liked to have made at their gaffers the other six days of the week.

The Doc amused them, made them more genial for some reason. His appearance seemed to help, coming as he did from the tradition of Scottish junior football inside-forwards, owing a great deal to stunted growth, a fondness for the bevvy, a disdain of sprinting more than six-yards and a body-swerve in which the heavily endowed backside and torso seemed to part company for a fraction of a second.

But he could play. He had deft touches which belied his appearance and that made him distinctive, set him apart.

Came the day of the cup-tie. The Vale were a club that folk talked about in Shettleston as if they were toffs because their name suggested something sylvan as opposed to us who had only wally-closes to brag about. And they had won the Scottish Junior Cup in the past, something that was never to be paraded up Shettleston main street.

It was windy. And I recall the pitch, after days without rain, was blowing 'stoor' into my face where I used to stand low down next to the perimeter railing, because in comparison to being in one of the larger Glasgow stadiums, this was like being at the coal-face where you could actually hear the grunts, the screams, the tirades, the obscenities as men hewed away at each to get something out of a game. I look back on junior football with genuine affection even though I realise that the passing of time has its romanticising effect. And, of course, I only have sketchy memories of that particular game. Although, Doc McManus's goal is in the mind as if it had been filmed and placed in my memory by Spielberg himself. It won the match after Shettleston had equalised a Vale lead and it came somewhere near the end of the game. The stats are shaky, the goal is not.

McManus was enduring the kind of game that was provoking some mirth among the Town support I recall. But they were tolerant of his lapses because as an eccentric, compared to his hardworking but mundane teammates he always carried the possibility of the unexpected even though at times he looked as threatening as the man who lined the pitch. The Town were playing towards the bottle-works end where many of the fans actually worked. Efforts were sailing over that bar as if the ball was volunteering to act as a plug for one of the bottles there. Then McManus struck.

The penalty area was packed and on the hard pitch the ball was frisky and awkwardly bouncing. It was about hip high when it came within his reach. As it fell he half-volleyed it. Yes, this rotund figure hit one of the most difficult of shots to control, as if he were of leonine stature, and the net obligingly stopped the ball from reaching the bottle-works. The game was won and the men behind me reacted as if the bookie had laid odds of 100–1 against him scoring at all.

I have no idea what the rest of life had in store for Doc. But although the name Shettleston Juniors is now defunct Doc is still an image that pops up occasionally to remind me of halcyon days when junior football seemed like one of the essential building blocks of nature.

3

Tribalism

Celtic v Rangers
3–1
League Cup
25 September 1948
Goal: Jackie Gallacher

PARTICULARLY ON SATURDAY nights a couple of us used to frequent the pavements in front of pubs along Shettleston Road to exploit the inebriated shapes that would emerge from the interiors, and fully aware of the basic good nature of Glasgow's East Enders, inflated by copious amounts of booze, knew they would often slip us a few pence, given the 'Buddy can you spare a dime' look on our faces of the underprivileged. That naked exploitation had another dimension to it because we would also hear gossip from men who seemed to miss nothing that mattered in life. We would choose either a Rangers or Celtic pub depending on recent results to exploit the mood of the denizens and so picked up the special lingo of the opposing affections. 'Which foot does he kick with?' seemed to be a prime sociological query. At that short-trousered age the two names that we heard talked about almost with reverence were 'Tully' and 'Thornton'. They were spoken of as disciples of contrasting faiths which we were never to take lightly. Thus, I consider myself fortunate enough to have seen them play against each other in a match at Celtic Park one clamorous day. I recall it also because I didn't pay to get in to my first Old Firm match. I was lifted over the turnstile by a complete stranger. Yes, this actually could happen in those days when welfare did not seem to emerge from legislation but came from the goodness of the heart. So

Charles Patrick Tully of Celtic and Willie Thornton of Rangers faced off against each other as specimens of Shettleston Road's split affiliations that made life worth living for so many. But, frankly, it was Tully's day. I had heard the chat about him like he had supernatural qualities as a player. The Belfast man I had only seen in photographs up till then looked more like the tousle-haired gasman who used to come to light up our tenement closes, and as menacing-looking as Bo Peep.

In Celtic Park that day though we learned a simple lesson for the growing-up process, that appearances can be deceptive. He glided through the game, audacity blending with skill. Upon such a balletic performance the Celtic recovery was based. For they were a goal down in only 11 mins from the foot of the high-scoring Willie Findlay of Rangers. Frequently Celtic teams in those times would wilt and succumb after such a set-back. But it was noticeable that, even then, they seemed to be having much of the play. And I do recall that stemmed principally because that tousled figure from Northern Ireland seemed to be everywhere. He was one of those players who the more he was able to slip past two or even three players could evoke admiration from his supporters although never really being in the hunt to score himself. Essentially that would not matter if he could prop up the others – which he did. He was the ultimate provider. In 39 minutes came the goal that changed the game and bolstered the Tully adulation. In a typical solo weaving movement he deceived a highly respected Rangers defence comprising of hardened players like George Young, 'Tiger' Shaw, Sammy Cox. Wrong footed and with a pass that his winger Johnny Paton accepted eagerly, that defence could not stop the ball being slipped to John Gallacher, in front of goal who had a relatively easy task of netting. 1–1.

Yes, Celtic would go on and score another two in their ultimate 3–1 victory. But that first goal, the equaliser, was a huge psychological boost for Celtic and I could sense it as a prelude to victory. For Rangers had never come across the likes of Tully before. The *Glasgow Herald* did not sell particularly well in my part of the world then. But those who did pick it up would have read this of that afternoon's result, 'The player who must take most of the blame or credit for that was Tully, undoubtedly the cleverest forward in the last 10 years of Scottish football.' The *Sunday Post* which most people read for the pictorial 'Broons' page, wrote this of the game, '...no matter what the records may show, this must always be remembered as Tully's match.'

Joe Mercer, who played against him as Arsenal's captain in the Coronation Cup final of 1953 and lost, once said, 'Who could forget Charlie? Marking him was an education.' And having put two corner kicks directly into the net at Brockville in 1953, after the first one had been disallowed, added further to his legend. Willie Thornton? Great players have 'off days' and this was one of them. I did recollect him hitting the post on one occasion but no more than that. Although, our takings outside the Rangers pub swelled later in the year as they were to go on and win the treble, with Willie Thornton their top-scorer with 34. But it was that Tully-inspired goal which inescapably reminds me of the day I was lifted over a turnstile.

4

Starstruck

Real Madrid v Eintracht Frankfurt
7–3
European Cup Final
18 May 1960 Hampden Park
Goal: Alfredo Di Stéfano

RIGHTLY OR WRONGLY this was the evening that encouraged me to think I could at least write something about football. How could I become entranced with what I watched in that game without wishing to register something about such a spectacle? Of course, I only toyed with the notion, as many others might have done as well. This game I relate, perhaps fancifully, to brotherhood. Now you become a naturalised Scottish citizen after five years lawful residence in the country. Ferenc Puskás, born in Budapest 1 April 1927, and Alfredo Di Stéfano, born in Buenos Aires in 1926, achieved it in exactly 90 minutes at the National Stadium in front of 127,621 witnesses who initially embraced the entire Real team as if they were relatives. Nature had helped. On a brilliantly sunny evening their white shirts looked as if they had been laundered by the gods. Indeed, in the years following, the Real players would look fondly back and admit that it was their finest performance in a match that some would claim was the greatest final ever played at that ground. But uniquely we all experienced something new in the crowd. We were simply spellbound. My good friend and superb journalist Hugh McIlvanney was to write in the *Observer* of 'the strong emotionalism that came over the crowd'. That was it. Although we were in awe of Real to an extent, because of their attempt to win this trophy for the fifth time in a row, the Germans had impressed us with the quality of their play in demolishing Rangers in the semi-finals, and actually scored first on the night. But, basically, at kick-off, there was no strong 'home' crowd sentiment for one or the other.

But there was contrast. Watching the Germans play before this game you could tell why the trains ran on time in their country. They were organised, strong and resolute. Real, on the other hand, offered the appearance of revellers who couldn't tell what time of day it was and cared less, but had boundless compensatory skills that were unleashed that night after being angered at losing the first goal. Now Ferenc Puskás was the only man ever to score four goals in a European final, as he did that night, encouraging the belief that the game 'belonged' to him. It was shared. The two goalscorers soared above the rest.

Real were already two goals up through Di Stéfano when just on the half-time whistle the ball was picked up on the left side of the penalty area by Puskás who, with his left foot, from the narrowest of angles, drove it high into the net with such ferocity I felt the crowd around me were almost gasping. That was 3–1. It cemented itself in my mind that a man with a right foot only for standing on could be so lethal.

In the 73rd minute Di Stéfano, the number 9 prominently on his shirt, but playing in a 'withdrawn' striker role and thus greatly influencing play all over the field, was to score a goal that effectively killed off the Germans, for it came only 60 seconds after Eintracht had reduced the margin to 6–2. The Germans had only the briefest of time to congratulate themselves before the Argentine punished them for such impudence. For me it stands out above the rest because of its single-mindedness, its calculated act of retribution for the Germans having the gall to score at all.

For the centre is taken with hasty indignation. Di Stéfano begins a run out of the centre-circle, head over the ball, touches it to Puskás who slips it back. And on the edge of the penalty area the ball leaves his right foot. It is so low it looks like it could scarify the pitch and, as it makes the net, the static goalkeeper looks as if he had simply been blinded by brilliance. The ecstatic crowd react for the first time like they are the 'home' pack right behind Real. The fact that Eintracht pulled one back to make the final score 7–3 was merely a statistical irrelevance. For that night, we as Scots, ought to have been reminded of our heritage. For we had invented the 'passing' game and exported it around the world, particularly to South America. Real were now playing it with such elegance that it seemed so alien to our standards. So we poured out of Hampden on that gloriously sunny evening so dazzled by the brilliance of it all that we little realised that Scottish football could rightly claim to have set the world on the creative footballing path we had just witnessed. And as educators we could rightly claim Alfredo Di Stéfano as one of our honorary graduates.

5

Pars for the Course

Scottish Cup Final Replay
26 April 1961
Celtic 0 v Dunfermline 2
Goal: Charlie Dickson

I WAS ATTRACTED to this game because I had started to write reports on football matches like a kind of hobby set apart from teaching the rudiments of the English language to kids, and admittedly with an arrogance that stemmed from disliking some of the reflections I was reading in the main Scottish newspapers at the time. And this game was a replay, with all of the intrigue associated with a provincial club, the 'Pars', taking on the favourites. It turned out to be something special. I definitely recall the word 'siege' being written in my unpublished account of the game. But, paradoxically, it was many years later in San Francisco in 1982 that I learned more about that renowned Celtic siege which had lent distinction to this final. I was enroute to New Zealand with the Scotland manager Jock Stein to assess our opposition in the forthcoming World Cup in Spain. We were met by a Celtic supporter who adored the former Celtic manager and had learned we were in town and offered to take us to see the renowned sights. In a café within sight of the Golden Gate Bridge he asked Stein a direct question. 'How did you feel about beating the club you loved in that final when you were in charge at Dunfermline?' To which a bemused Stein replied, 'I would have felt worse if I had lost!' Which was a kinder way of saying, 'I was always in this business to win things. For God's sake, what else is there?' And then he went on to talk about one man, Eddie Connachan. He was the Dunfermline goalkeeper on that rain-sodden pitch when the ball was like the proverbial bar of wet-soap. The Fifers had gone one up against the run of play in the second half when in the 67th minute Dave Thomson bent low to head a cross from the left by George Peebles past Frank Haffey in the Celtic goal.

Then followed the siege. Celtic armed with men like Paddy Crerand, Willie Fernie, John Hughes, Stevie Chalmers were barely ever out of the Dunfermline half. In circumstances like these the media along with the vast majority in the 87,866 crowd felt the equaliser was inevitable. However, those of us who were there can still recall the amazing series of saves that Connachan made that day. He was an ex-miner like the Dunfermline manager himself and that might have created a special affinity, for by and large Stein was allergic to goalkeepers throughout his career as they seemed to bring rushes of contrasting emotions to his head. That day Connachan stood up to the battering like he was facing a dam bursting. He threw himself around the goal-line, he clutched, he palmed, he tipped, he smothered, and in one particular instance he miraculously blocked a 25-yard Crerand shot through a ruck of players that had looked bound for the net.

William Shakespeare in penning his plays would, to great effect, use a device called tragicomedy. He would have been in his element that day in describing the ending which evoked tears and laughter all in the one, depending on your point of view. It is what made the goal so memorable. A long innocuous ball is played towards the Celtic goal in the 88th minute. It was straightforwardly a goalkeeper's ball. Except it wasn't. Frank Haffey was in the Celtic goal. He fumbled the ball, and when it dropped to his feet, for some unaccountable reason he seemed to walk past it like it was contaminated. Charlie Dickson, an honest-to-God kind of striker was left to walk the ball into the empty net adopting the casual demeanour of an owner escorting his dog for a pee. 2–0. Close to time up, some disillusioned Celtic supporters vented their fury at the outcome by throwing bottles aimlessly but dangerously into space. My researcher Pat Woods and father at the bottom of the terracing were paralysed by the terror of it all. Dunfermline had won the 76th final in their 76th year.

A man in a white coat rushed on to the field to hug his players with a special embrace. It was Stein. I now recall that manoeuvre as merely a dress-rehearsal for other triumphs to come, and of which my reports of such would then be in the public domain.

6

Auditioning

Celtic v Rangers
0–1
Scottish First Division
8 September 1962
Goal: Willie Henderson

IT WAS WRITING a short story for the BBC which had nothing to do with football that introduced me to sports broadcasting. Liking what they heard of my reading it on the air they asked me if I would be interested in reporting on football. However, they would have to audition me and could I pick a game and come back in so they could listen to how I could cope with such reporting? I chose the Old Firm game. There was also Shettleston Juniors versus the Bens I could have provided for their delectation, and how I could cleverly make a silk-purse out of a pig's ear, sort of thing. But this was an audition I was heading for, and doesn't an Old Firm match speak for itself? Yes, in crude terms admittedly, and with unique choral accompaniments, but it would be all too easy. The game would do the job for me.

I got more than I had bargained for. Would they allow me to exceed the two minutes they asked for? Like, half an hour? I would have needed it.

Firstly, how do you describe being part of a crowd of 72,000 rooted in visceral hatred. Would I need to reflect on that in some way and make some philosophical reference to knee-deep sectarianism? But, this was the BBC I was auditioning for, who certainly at that time had nothing more provocative on the air than the blessed voice of Kathleen Garscadden introducing *Children's Hour*. Play safe, was my uppermost thought.

Although, the crowd itself gave me another story because 19 fans were injured that day when they stormed the Janefield Street entrance in their anxiety to gain entry before kick-off. Another two ended up in hospital having ribs crushed against a barrier inside the ground.

The two incidents which made my biro skid along the surface of the notebook and put me in Hemingway mode, was, of course, the goal. And certainly the penalty award. It came on the half-hour after inconclusive and reasonably balanced play. Paddy Crerand in midfield for Celtic and frustrated by the inept play in front of him, strode into Rangers penalty area, where he was clearly tripped by Ralph Brand. The penalty awarded was incontestable. But the Rangers players began to complain about how Crerand was placing the ball on the spot, apparently generously, to his advantage and kept pestering him about it until he lost the rag and threw the ball at his opponents as if offering them to spot it. After that furore it was no surprise that Ritchie in goal saved his eventual shot.

Such an event, unsurprisingly, gives enormous boost to one obvious side and although Celtic had much of the play in the second half, they never really convinced me they were going to score, and definitely Rangers looked the more dangerous on the counter. Then it came. Willie Henderson was a figure the Ibrox fans held in high regard. Small, wiry, tricky and with excellent judgement of pace he had been quietish but still potentially threatening until near seven minutes from the end. For some reason he had switched to the unaccustomed left-wing of Rangers attack and in one thrust beat Duncan MacKay at right-back, made towards goal and shot. Now, my recollection is that it was not a cannonball Haffey had to deal with but merely let it slip through his grasp, and although defender Kennedy tried to stop its gentle roll towards the line he could only succeed in helping it on his way. The winner. 1–0. I was so pleased to have a goal to describe I decorated it with language fit for a World Cup final. At the end of the audition the anonymous BBC man said, 'We'll let you know!'

7

In at the Death

Third Lanark v Hibernian
1–4
Scottish First Division
Cathkin Park
3 November 1962
Goal: Jim Scott

THE BBC SET me free to do my first ever television commentary that day. I was too nervous to have any great expectations but I was travelling to a stadium that I greatly loved. When I was a boy my grandfather would take me on a long bus trip nearly every Saturday from the other side of Glasgow to see the Hi-Hi at Cathkin, because he thought Jimmy Mason, their dapper inside-forward, who was part of our conquering post-war Wembley side at Wembley on April 9 1949 and scored the opening goal in our 3–1 victory, was the greatest player on the planet. Mason was on my mind as I climbed onto a television platform for the first time, at the top of their long sloping terracing opposite their stand, for Thirds were on a slippy financial slope at the time and it was difficult to relate quality such as Mason to a club whom many thought were doomed. They had an owner in Bill Hiddleston who turned out to have run this respected institution in the south-side of the city like a speakeasy in south-side Chicago. He was a fraudster with astonishing nerve.

So rumours abounded about financial problems for the home club as Thirds and Hibs took to the field and my mike felt like I was lifting the weighty Stone of Destiny.

You could not see the Hibs jerseys without thinking of their Famous

Five, and football people from the east in particular kept their memory rightfully alive. History, though, can sometimes weigh contemporary players down in the constant refrains that can be heard about the past records and any subsequent Hibs side simply had to live with that paradoxical factor. But, thankfully for the Hibs supporters, later that night, they had a glimpse of their great past. For on the film shown on *Sportsreel* (as our programme was entitled then), they heard me for the first time, as I raised the decibels by describing a goal that any Hibs player of any generation would have considered one of the best.

The odd aspect is that Thirds seemed the better side for much of the game but even in my rookie state I never felt they could capitalise on their midfield superiority. Then came the moment a goal was scored that made me feel I had arrived as a commentator. So, unsurprisingly, I gave it, as we would say in the trade, 'laldy'.

Jim Scott finds the ball at his feet close to the centre-circle and takes off as if he has decided that any useful help was not going to be forthcoming. Now I can't recall how many men he swayed and tricked past. Perhaps, three or four. By the time he had completed his mini-tour of the pitch all he had remaining to do was the easy part. He slipped it past the keeper nonchalantly. His big brother Alex Scott who was still playing for Rangers at the time would have been envious of one of the goals of the year. Despite that clear win, Hibs were only able to finish in 16th place in the league by the end of the season.

What I could not have known at the time was that it would be the last time I commentated at Cathkin. And that I had a goal to treasure that would always remind me of a great ground. It effectively closed down after Drew Busby scored their last ever goal in their heavy 5–1 defeat against Dumbarton at Boghead on Friday 28 April 1967. The Scott goal though was the first that put my exaggerated voice into the public domain which on reflection must have sounded like a hammy actor trying to recite Shakespeare. That's how it felt as I walked away from a commentating platform for the first time. But I had at least laid my voice down there before they had put up the shutters on treasured space that I had always associated with growing pains and highly expectant bus-trips around the city.

8

Nobody Does It Better

England v Scotland
1–2
Home International
6 April 1963
Goal: Jim Baxter

IT WAS NOTICEABLE that Jim Baxter only put water to his lips as he and his partner sat beside my wife and I at the Variety Club Ball in Glasgow in the winter of 2000. We had been warned in advance that he was a 'changed man' by several people. Nevertheless, that did not prepare us for encountering a mere husk of the man I had known in the previous years when he could make a football seem like a serf in his continual acts of mesmeric control of opponents. Of course like many others we had known of his reputation for putting away booze with the same kind of determination that took Edmund Hillary to the top of Everest. And now he was paying the price for lavish self-indulgence having had to end his career at the age of 31. So in terms of conversation I felt like I was handling a delicate piece of porcelain and that by saying the wrong word I might end up with fragments on my hands.

I took the safe route by reminding him of the first time I saw him in a Scotland jersey when I was a fledgling broadcaster. It was Wembley in 1963, in front of a crowd of 98,606. Although I had little to do that day in radio I admitted to him that I was nevertheless suffering a little from stage fright and that what he achieved that afternoon was like turning my frayed nerves into sinews of steel. I could see that he was interested because I had picked, unwittingly, a game that he believed had been overshadowed by another event he was more colourfully associated with. That was the defeat of the World Champions England in 1967 in the same stadium when he had played keepie-uppie with the ball in the middle of match like a boy up a wally-close in Glasgow, to the disgust of the humiliated English and the rapturous delight of the tartan hordes. No. He was adamant that the game that he closeted affectionately in his memory was 1963.

I witnessed how a man recognised principally as an entertainer, a showman, a manipulator, a tormentor on the park became a leader, an example of grit and determination with the artistry held in abeyance, not deserted. For Scotland lost their captain Eric Caldow after only five minutes with a leg broken in two places in a clash with the England striker Bobby Smith and in the days before substitutions had to play out the game with only ten men. Baxter's position in the middle of the field meant he was rarely out of touch with the play and the others around him like Dave Mackay, Denis Law, John White responded to his promptings. Nothing gallus. Everything was with a sense of purpose.

Now he was not a noted goalscorer although in his 359-game career he did net 37 times which meant the well was never completely dry. But although I saw few of these goals I am willing to bet that the one he achieved in the 28th minute at Wembley was his greatest.

It was with the left foot. His brain and that foot had an obvious grudge against the right, which was left mostly as a spectator to events. So at that moment with Scotland giving a good account of themselves despite their ten-man disadvantage they needed confirmation of their mounting ascendancy.

Baxter takes the ball from midfield, swerves past opponents to the edge of the penalty area and despite the apparent leisurely manner unleashes a bulleted shot to the roof of the net. A Scottish goal at any time at Wembley is a cause for celebratory relief. This time it carried a stamp of individual brilliance that presaged overall victory. Yes, two minutes later Baxter sent the goalkeeper the wrong way in taking a penalty for his second in a comparative blink of an eye. But it was that left-foot blend of control and power that initiated Scotland's eventual 2–1 triumph and inspired an evening, as I was reliably informed, of bacchanalian revelry by Baxter and friends.

On the back of that he became the man about town. With a Fife accent thicker than the Arctic ice cap, he was tattooing his name over a city with deeds of style on the park and legends of socialising off it. He was the talk of the steamie! Without any difficulty you could bump into someone who claimed to have seen him with an attractive companion and looking two sheets to the wind. I began to think that if you didn't have a Baxter story to tell you were almost a social recluse.

Legitimacy for his lifestyle stemmed from what he did on the park which was with a distinctive emphasis on style. The man who brought him to Ibrox from Kirkcaldy, Scott Symon, with his kirk-elder-like view on life, bore the gossip and rumours like a father hearing stories of a son surviving in the trenches, but with gritted-teeth tolerance because Baxter was producing the goods. But there was one day when he produced them in such a way that Symon went almost berserk.

It was at Hampden on a 15 May evening in 1963. The Scottish Cup final replay. The final itself on 4 May had ended in a 1–1 draw in an uneventful match. To many that was a surprise, because Rangers had dominated the second half but found Haffey in goal unbeatable. For this replay we had left the wind and rain of a Saturday behind and the sunny, balmy spring evening was the perfect inducement for Baxter to impose his will on the match. It was the Davie Wilson goal in that game to make it 2–0 that saw Celtic crumbling. It was the take-off point for Baxter to put on his own personal show.

He then shunted the game into a lay-by of self-indulgence. He would take the ball to the touchline and juggle with it. He would put his foot on it and invite the tackle like a man in a public park cavorting with a puppy. And at one stage he simply sat on the ball in the ultimate gesture of contempt. But frustration was growing on the bench and around the Rangers legions who had never forgotten how their great rivals had historically hammered them 7–1 in October 1957. They felt this was now an opportunity for revenge against such a weak Celtic team. The final score was in fact 3–0 to Rangers with Brand scoring his second 20 minutes from the end.

But as the Rangers players trooped into the dressing room after the match they were met by an incensed manager who went straight to his captain Bobby Shearer who was expecting a hug. Instead, he faced a tirade. 'What right had you to humiliate these Celtic players? That was outrageous! The supporters wanted more goals!' Symon screamed. Bobby was to say to me in later years, 'The manager treated Jim differently from the rest of us. He had to get at him through me. If you had this talent I suppose you become a law unto yourself.'

Shearer, a Lanarkshire man of solid values, was also, clearly, like others, a page at Baxter's court. Now, perforce, teetotal, the Fifer left the ball early that night in 2000 and afterwards I realised I had treated him with what he was probably due. As a sick relative in his last days. He died a few months later.

9

A Winning Head

Scotland v England
1–0
11 April 1964
Goal: Alan Gilzean

EVEN THOUGH SCOTTISH international football was riding an apparent crest at the time I was still nervous climbing the steep stairs to the commentary positions high above the Hampden pitch on that day. My own personal situation added to the tension. For I was still a schoolteacher at the time and on Monday morning pupils were not slow to inform me of stumbles, mispronunciations, mistaken identities and what special affiliation I had with any particular club. We were certainly all on the one side when we took on the Auld Enemy. However they would always find something critical to say. Well, as a teacher hadn't I always encouraged them to be creative and outspoken?

Then there was the fact that this would be my first BBC engagement with this great fixture. I was still an apprentice in broadcasting and painfully feeling so. I had enjoyed watching Scotland in recent times and just consider the names I had to conjure with that day, Greig, McNeill, Baxter, Law – just a sample of the talent on show on the Scotland side. And hadn't they done well in recent times? Scotland were actually seeking a successive hat-trick of victories over their great rivals in this traditional match. The Scottish newspapers I read before travelling to the game were playing that up madly, although typically with addendums that betrayed the usual circumspect manner with which we always approached this special game.

There was also a comparative newcomer to the squad called Alan Gilzean who had appeared in the colours for the first time in 1963. I had watched him play at club level for Dundee, who were a powerful force in the land at the time, having won the Scottish League Championship in 1961/2 season and reached the semi-finals of the European Cup in 1963. He was especially gifted in and around the penalty area. His speed and instinct for being in the right place at the right time was a major factor in Dundee's emergence as a powerful force as he was to score 169 goals in 190 games for them. And of course, he was specially talented in the air. What we did begin to realise was that English scouts were travelling to Dundee and a' the airts in bus-loads, to measure his prowess. Rumours abounded as to who might nab him and I do know some Glasgow journalists who felt he might end up at one of the Old Firm, although that parochial thinking is ingrained in my city.

I wondered how he would fare in the kind of company I have already mentioned. My recollection is he looked at first overawed by finding himself in this exalted company. He was there and thereabouts without unduly bothering the English defence. Most of the penetration came from the Rangers pair on the wings Henderson and Wilson, and Law in the middle, but the competence and organisational influence of Bobby Moore in the heart of the English defence neutralised most of the Scottish attacks. *The Times* actually reported in recognition of that, 'Here Moore, supported firmly by Norman, played a giant part in his role of sweeper at the back... more than once denying the volatile Law or darting Henderson the goal that for so long looked imminent.'

But when it did come it was with a simplicity that also perfectly illustrated Gilzean's aerial judgement. Eighteen minutes to go Davy Wilson took a corner on the left. Gilzean simply outjumped an erstwhile immaculate England defence to glide the ball with the left side of his head into the net, and I almost choked on my words up high in the radio commentary area where I was doing summaries. There was no holding back the Scotland supporters' right to boast of the 'hat-trick'. In retrospect it is also sad to realise that two great headers of a football in that same game, Billy McNeill and Alan Gilzean, were to die of negative brain conditions. It is only now, decades later, that we are beginning to be alerted to consider that in our sport, there has been dutiful sacrifice. So that goal by Alan Gilzean could be considered not just a statistic in a game, but an act of valour.

10

End of an Era

Celtic v Kilmarnock
3–2
Scottish Cup
6 March 1965
Goal: John Hughes

THERE WAS CHARGED emotion in the air. It was the end of an era. Two major figures, of whom much in Scottish football had already been written, would be in competition for the last time. Jimmy McGrory, the Celtic manager was giving way to the ex-miner from Blantyre called Stein, and Willie Waddell had announced that at the end of the season he would be leaving his post as manager of Kilmarnock. In their different ways they were titanic figures as players. McGrory was probably one of the finest ever centre-forwards and is the all-time leading goalscorer in British football having scored 550 goals in 547 appearances.

Waddell, or 'Deedle' as he was affectionately known, was a renowned winger who only ever played for one senior club, Rangers, and in that time was a major influence who helped his club win four league titles and two Scottish Cups and also played eight times for his country. They both had gone into management eventually at different periods. McGrory had to experience a largely barren time with the club although could boast of one of the biggest ever cup final wins, when they overwhelmed Rangers 7–1 in the Scottish League Cup final on 19 October 1957.

This was his last day after almost two decades in charge. There were mixed emotions in the crowd of 47,00. McGrory, for all that he was deeply respected by the large following, had not brought the degree of success that might have been expected from such a major club. Generally, under McGrory's management, they had been inferior to Rangers in that austere post-war period. However, expectancy flavoured the air, as a new exciting figure, who already had solid achievements to his name, was about to takeover. For me, McGrory was simply one of the most genial managers I ever had dealings with. Polite, always approachable and forthcoming, I also had to consider, paradoxically, that he was simply too nice a man in that role to be fussy about formalities and was always accessible. For instance, that day, which must have been deeply emotional for him, I went to the Celtic dressing room door, knocked it and was surprised that he opened it himself and instantly agreed to come out for us to film he and Waddell together.

The Kilmarnock manager was testier about my request and I thought I was going to have problems, but after informing him that McGrory had agreed, he relented and they both stood with me on the track at Celtic Park as I filmed them for posterity shaking the hands that both had been used plentifully in the past lifting trophies. But, as they left me, I had to wonder how the Celtic players, not without their trenchant critics, would respond. What kind of send-off would it be?

Killie were a real force at that time under Waddell and there was no assumption that it would be easy for Celtic. So although Lennox had scored in 15 minutes and the Ayrshire men had equalised in the second-half only for Bertie Auld to put them ahead only a minute later, the game demanded something special. It came in the 67th minute with the score 2–1. It was from an Auld cross and the powerful head of 'Yogi', John Hughes. It was that big fellow who provided the perfect facsimile that reminded the fans of their past history, bulleting the ball past the keeper in spectacular fashion for the third goal. It could not have been more appropriate an ending to the last goal under McGrory's stewardship. For that is the way he used to finish off opponents himself with powerful neck muscles that seemed to give him the power of a Brahman Bull. He was now, as manager, handing over to a former centre-half who as a player could only kick a ball properly with his left foot. Fortunately for the Celtic support he had other assets.

11

Decimal Points

Hearts v Kilmarnock
0–2
24 April 1965
Winning of Championship
Goal: Brian McIlroy

I WAS NEVER good at maths. It was to the despair of my father who felt that mastery of figures was the only way to guide you successfully through life. So one notable day in 1965, about to set out to commentate on an important football match, I impressed him with a seeming alacrity with figures. Actually, someone else had worked them out for me. I think I can recall much of what I said to him. It went like, 'Look! Hearts are two points in front at the top of the league. If Killie are to win the title they will have to score two goals and not concede any. Hearts, only need a draw to take the title. All this is because you divide the total goals scored in the season by the goals against you get a kind of average. So if Killie did get their two goals they would win the title by 0.042 of a goal.'

So I arrived at Tynecastle that beautiful spring day, with renewed respect from my father, and with the sun making Auld Reekie palatable to an inveterate Glaswegian who was also aware of certain difficulties facing a commentator in that stadium. In those days there were pillars holding up the 'shed' enclosure which inevitably got in the way of clear recordings and the efforts of the cameramen to minimise their presence would have drawn the praise of skilled snipers. So we had our own personal tension to contend with. And I personally emphasised on the air – I suppose selfishly – that we were at THE grand finale, because at the same time on the other side of the country Jock Stein was leading his new club Celtic to a Scottish Cup Final against Dunfermline. We were not to be overshadowed!

The game itself met all the circumstances of a great conclusion. The play flowed seemingly evenly until 17 minutes before half-time when the diminutive Tommy McLean just inside the penalty area chipped a ball to the far post, where the unattended Dave Sneddon headed Killie into the lead. At 0–1 the decimal point in the stats was beginning to wobble. But which way would it eventually end up with such a long period still to play? That query and anxiety still in most Killie minds was eased somewhat when after Hearts had carelessly squandered possession in midfield, the ball was picked up by Bertie Black whose incisive pass was collected by Brien McIlroy who sent a low shot past goalkeeper Cruickshank to make it 2–0 with the whole of the second-half still to come. With Hearts needing only a goal to win the title, much of the rest of the game was a siege on Ferguson in the Killie goal. He was brilliant. Indeed, just before the end came the moment that classically snatched the word 'Goal' from my lips. The moment when Hearts could have/should have won the title.

Alan Gordon, the tall fair-haired Hearts striker was left in front of goal and looked certain to score with only Ferguson to beat. It is perhaps too easy to say he froze, but I certainly would not dismiss the thought. He certainly did not strike the ball properly and the keeper thwarted the effort. The striker must have known that, too readily, he would be cast as the villain of the afternoon. Some consequences like that are inevitable in this business and it aggravated him for years after.

But that McIlroy goal not only won a title. I also recall it as the turning point for Waddell who rushed onto the field in the white coat hugging his players knowing that he was relinquishing his post whatever the result might have been. But the success – the title he had engineered – meant that his immediate career as a journalist after that day could not survive the call from Ibrox in 1969 who, with the onset of Stein, were then looking for Churchillian inspiration. McIlroy had cleared the pitch for him.

For myself I ended the day drinking with our camera crew in an Edinburgh hostelry in celebration of the fact we had given the public a clear view of historic events, despite the pillars.

12

An Italian Dessert

Scotland v Italy
1–0
World Cup Qualifier
9 November 1965
Goal: John Greig

THE GREATEST VALUE of an Italian restaurant for me, during my career, was not just the cuisine, a weekly gorge of which was needed to keep me sane, but the bubbly chat about football. Every Italian waiter I encountered had something worthwhile to say about the beautiful game. After all, *catenaccio* could have been a Tuscan soup for all I knew, until a couple of nights before that Scotland–Italy World Cup qualifier. I was in my favourite spot, *Da Luciano* in Bothwell, just outside Glasgow. In conversation with Toni, the head waiter, he demonstrated what *catenaccio* meant using bread-rolls and a bottle of Chianti my wife and I were about to destroy – the rolls surrounding the bottle in serried ranks that somehow or other I had to accept was the defensive system the Italians were likely to play against Scotland. In English the word meant, 'door-bolt' which left little to the imagination as to what it was intended create. Toni seemed to know his stuff and as a rookie in broadcasting who had been assigned to radio duties for this particular game, alongside the star radio commentator of those times, Douglas Lowe, I was willing to listen to anybody to pick up any morsel for use on the air.

However, someone else was there that night. He was a man who shared my affection for this restaurant. He was Joe Beltrami, at that time Scotland's foremost criminal solicitor. He was rarely off the pages of our main newspapers, given the less than charming lives many of my compatriots led in our land. We would cross paths frequently there, and in being increasingly recognised as a purveyor of the Scottish game on television, I was often assailed by him offering his views on Scottish football – particularly about his beloved Celtic. He took unkindly to any criticism of the club he supported and was never slow to inform me of his perceived deficiencies on my part. He had heard me talking with Toni about the Italy game and unsurprisingly moved in to have his say as he was always eager to do. His favourite target was the SFA which he believed merely echoed views and sentiments emanating from Ibrox. And clearly he was not happy with the relatively new Celtic boss Jock Stein taking on a part-time role with this suspect institution, as national manager, given the task he faced at Parkhead in the objective of replacing Rangers as the dominant force in Scottish football. His voice boomed over the restaurant as if he were turning the diners into a jury listening to the grilling of some guilty party. It was both provocative and stimulating and I wouldn't have missed our encounters for the world. Here was a prominent figure putting our football into a perspective that indicated that the domestic rivalry between our two major clubs was more engaging and significant than any other form of football. Of course, he wasn't the only man who held such a view but since he put his trenchant opinions into my ears so frequently he was like a self-appointed invigilator of my broadcasting utterances, although, thankfully, choosing that civilised haven of good food and superb Italian wine that lessened the notion that he was putting me on the witness stand.

So, there I was entering the commentary box at Hampden Park that night, nervous and beset, annoyingly, by thoughts of these two encounters at *Da Luciano*. Were the Italians really going to be all that defensive? Really? And were Scotland competing not simply with Italy but with a sizeable element in our land obsessed more with the outcome of domestic football?

Now Jock Stein had burst on the scene like a revolutionary seeking to uproot the weary conventions of the game and having taken clubs from outside Glasgow to cup wins, beaten European oppositions as well, and won Celtic a cup after only weeks in the post, had accepted the temporary role of Scotland manager in tandem with his Parkhead berth. In that SFA role he had started well with a creditable 1–1 draw in Poland and then suffered two defeats in a row including that harrowing Poland disaster at home, when the visitors scored two goals in the last couple of minutes of the game to win 2–1 and the complimentary expression 'Stein's Stunners' took on a new slant. He had at least shown he was his own man by dropping the highly popular Jim Baxter from that last game and indicated he would not take any advice from the hacks! As for this game I felt that Joe Beltrami might make play of the fact that when Stein's team was announced it had five Rangers players to Celtic's two, including Bobby Murdoch making his international debut. Although, the player Stein had left out of the Poland game, Jim Baxter, was made captain against Italy, in one of the selections that Stein knew would puzzle the hacks. At that stage all I could read into the players he had chosen was that he wanted to win this game badly, given his own desire to reach new horizons. And these were men he knew well regardless of club identity. They would give their all.

His opponents would not be travelling to Hampden in November with any great qualms since their defensive strategy was, I assumed, ingrained in their make-up. All they required after all was a draw, which was right up their *strada*. Two of their names were well enough known in Scotland. Gianni Rivera, of AC Milan, whom the Italian press called 'Golden Boy' and who was to win the Ballon d'Or in 1969 as one of the greatest European players ever. And the moustachioed Sandro Mazzola of Inter on the left who at speed was a blur.

And there was John Greig. Good times or bad, for Scotland or for his club, he always seemed to be everywhere on the field when it mattered. He personified upright commitment which although viewed from the other side of the city Stein nevertheless admired. In that year Greig was beginning to create the model of stability that would become legendary in the Scottish game. That night would add considerably to his reputation. At kick-off I thought about the bread-rolls and the Chianti again as the Italians began to spray the ball about with the alacrity of players who had left *catenaccio* behind in Italy. To me this was a more aggressive Italian side than I had expected. However, the floodlights at Hampden in those times lent an atmosphere that would have suited a funeral cortege. The murkiness was commensurate with our growing frustration in the radio commentary position. Billy Bremner was man-marking Rivera, John Greig who had made two great goal-line clearances in the early part of the game was more prominent than captain Baxter whose wiles were clearly well enough known but easily negated by the Italians. I was beginning to feel we would do well to get away with a goalless draw. But a Scottish goal now seemed as unlikely as Toni serving us haggis any time at *Da Luciano*.

Then, wonderment. With two minutes to go, Greig took a slick pass from his so far inept colleague Baxter. A pass that was redemption for himself and others around. He had stroked the ball into Greig's path. Instinct then took over. He struck at it from just inside the penalty area, and as he did so it looked no more than any of the other situations we had been in before that had come to nothing. Except, this time, we saw it bulge the net. The sheer incredulity that struck us perhaps made it appear more spectacular than it actually was. But it was decorated with so much meaning that we were almost struck dumb and in the commentary box there was an initial silence followed by almost childish wonderment. 1–0. *Catenaccio* unbolted. A national triumph. Even Joe with all his forensic legal skills would have found it difficult to defend anyone who had reacted to that astonishing climax with indifference.

13

Camera Chaos

Rangers v Kilmarnock
6–4
Scottish League Cup Semi-Final
6 October 1965
Goal: Tommy McLean

I was introduced to the incandescent rage of the public for the first time while shopping in the Co-op the morning after I had just completed one of my early television commentaries. The man with white whiskers who looked as if he had done service in Flanders fields didn't hold back. 'What the f... happened last night?' He was referring to the fact that a Scottish League Cup semi-final between Rangers and Kilmarnock which had ended 6–4 for Rangers appeared on our screens to have been a 1–1 draw. He was accusing us of a fix, in not letting us see all the Rangers goals. Although I was deeply embarrassed, I tried to explain to him some of the technicalities of filming football with two 16mm cameras, not the big electronic outside-broadcasting cameras we all now take for granted. It was my first encounter with a dissatisfied customer and naively I tried to put up a case like I was a Philadelphia lawyer defending the purity of public service broadcasting without then understanding that when viewers had made up their minds about bias of any sort in broadcasting, nothing can budge them. In truth, putting any game of football on the screen in those days was pure adventure when it was with film cameras.

Now in this game I was to commentate on ten goals, two hat-tricks and a feisty second-half fightback by Killie. So as a novice I felt like a pauper who had snuck into a Christmas banquet and willingly tucked in. What more could you want as a young commentator? At the same time I was decidedly uneasy when I thought of the circumstances. The game was scheduled to finish at 9.15pm approx. Our programme *Sportsreel* was to start at 11pm. Since we were using film cameras, the reels had to be taken from the ground to a lab to be firstly processed then transported to the BBC and put into the hands of a film editor. Beside me on the platform was the eyes and ears of the game. He was an assistant producer who had a notebook in his hand and was there to record any incident of note, goals, fouls, near misses, and with the times of each of these duly recorded. It was vital for the film editor to know where he had to put his razor-blade through the film which came to him or else he would be working in the dark, more than literally so. And woe-betide us all if that man could not read the writing in the notebook. It was as fragile as that. And then there was the camera crew.

They were not specialists in football. They were experienced and skilled in all areas outside a football stadium. This particular crew did documentary filming of high quality but far removed from trying to follow a ball in the murkiness of Hampden Park. Although, when I identified my first goal, Rangers' George McLean scoring with a rising shot in 12 minutes, I also noticed a flutter among the camera crew. I knew something was up. I also understood that any existing malevolence could be in the film cameras themselves. They could easily take the huff and jam. You could see a cameraman at times acting like he had been stung by a bee, his camera hanging limp, like in post-coital droop, incapable of anymore. There was a young assistant cameraman there whose very agitation around the cameras suggested that the torrent of goals I was commentating on might not make it into the public view. A lad who was to go on to greater things. I ploughed on nevertheless.

Put all these complications together and you had our presenter of *Sportsreel* Peter Thomson becoming renowned as the master apologist. Perhaps every week he had to stand in front of a camera and try to explain to the Scottish public why there were glaring flaws in our output. What helped the ease with which he delivered the bad news was that on the opposing channel STV, Arthur Montford was being compelled to act exactly the same way in this common weakness of technical inadequacies.

So what did the public miss that night? Two hat-tricks scored by the McLeans, George for Rangers and Tommy for Kilmarnock. But what really made the night was the Killie fightback when they were 6–1 down.

The wee winger from Rugby Park who was later to star for Rangers was outstanding and I made him the Man of the Match for having the skill and temerity to score three goals in those last 20 minutes and which I played up to the highest volume. You cannot imagine how deprived you can feel when all that effort you have put into reflecting an exceptional game, lies perished somewhere along that complicated route to the screen. I have no idea where exactly it failed this time. Perhaps it was a combination of factors. The only goal that I can recall made the air was the Tommy McLean penalty awarded after Kai Johansen had brought him down. I saw that go out on the air which is why it can be listed in my recollection.

So did anything useful come out of that night? Yes. That young assistant cameraman that night at Hampden I mentioned, I met many years later on a flight to New York. He actually invited me into where he was sitting in first-class. Bill Forsyth was off to discuss making a film in Hollywood. I am convinced his beautiful film *Gregory's Girl* about the footballing girl was inspired by his trying to make amends for the missing goals of Hampden that night. For in that film at least he made sure we saw the football. And the moral for me from that night? If you have trouble in a broadcast never stand in a Co-op queue the following day.

14

A Foreign Foot

Rangers v Celtic
1–0
Scottish Cup Final Replay
27 April 1966
Goal: Kai Johansen

Although Hamlet might be thought of as the Great Dane, among the Rangers fraternity that entitlement is in constant dispute as they reminisce about two men deserving of the title. Brian Laudrup or Kai Johansen? Both of them took to Scottish life as if they came from no further east than Peterhead. The first one I saw in action was Johansen. I was still relatively new to broadcasting at that time and I always felt honoured to be asked to sit beside the great radio commentator Douglas Lowe on the Saturday of the first game. In fact, as I can recall, I believe I was somewhat overawed sitting in the high press-box looking down on a crowd of 126,599 when Rangers and Celtic were joint top of the league. I remember Lowe, with great experience, saying to me at the end of the goalless draw that the Old Firm matches can sometimes be fraught with fear of defeat and that we had just witnessed a perfect example of that in a largely featureless encounter.

I was back in midweek almost as if I had matured over the weekend and didn't quite feel I was a raw novitiate. But I did know that Celtic had gone into this game with the media around me making them favourites. Stein was making a huge impression on all of us with his transformative spirit that meant many of them had to toe the line, for example, as he would shut the door on them if they didn't turn up on time for press conferences but spoke with an authority that was in stark contrast to the evasive and somewhat aloof Scot Symon on the other side of the city. In terms of enlightenment about the game Stein was taking the pundits' fancy.

When you look back on a final with only one goal it tends to obscure everything else. All the intricacies, manoeuvres, tactics are subordinated to a single recollection with all the rest shunted out. But in fact it was a superior game to the first match and Celtic certainly flourished but without a cutting edge. They were faced by solidity where veteran Jimmy Millar was played in midfield for Rangers and provided experience and belief that clearly was infectious among his colleagues. They had also replaced Jim Forrest with George McLean in the striking role.

All this attention on striking potential, on either side, also heightened the special circumstances under which the goal was scored and why it was so memorable. None of the acknowledged strikers were within yards of the ball. It came in the 70th minute from an unexpected source. It came with stunning effect because nobody expected anything menacing that came from a ball loosely played out of the Celtic defence. The blue-shirted figure there finding the ball unexpectedly at his feet, totally unmarked, was able to stride forward unchallenged, and from about 25 yards out suddenly let fly.

Now Kai Johansen was the kind of player, as a right-back, whose play on the field mirrored what he was like as a man. Neat, precise, fair-minded, sincere commitment to a task. He did his job without any flamboyance and he was clearly treasured as a defender, above all. For in 158 appearances for Rangers he only ever scored 4 goals. But then, unlike the modern full-back, he kept conventionally within his defensive shell. Not that night though. His shot was with controlled venom and accuracy and few keepers would have been able to thwart it.

The following day a picture appeared in all the newspapers, front and back. It showed Johansen totally unmarked in the distance with Ronnie Simpson lying helpless with the ball bulging the net. The picture itself and the words in print could not convey the stunning effect this had on Hampden with an eruption from the Rangers end that I think was a mix of elation and surprise.

This had a cruel consequence for a single player. John Hughes, 'Yogi', of Celtic spoke to me years later about it. It was a sad and almost embittered account of that incident. Stein had turned his fury on Hughes after the game and accused him of losing the cup for Celtic since he had been given strict instructions to cover Johansen rigidly whenever Rangers were in possession. Hughes explained to me why he thought that was grossly unfair.

'We had gone to Seamill for the build up of the game. It was during training that I felt my hamstring going. There was something there tightening up and I knew I wasn't going to be fully fit. I told Jock but he kept saying, "You'll be all right, you'll make it", since he knew I had always played well against Johansen. Now I curse myself for not standing up to him and saying outright that the hamstring would hold me back as it did. He was a difficult man to stand up to. I suppose it was because of the fear of him that many players had. You could say he persuaded me to play, but in fact he actually made it impossible for me to say "No!".'

The night certainly belonged to Rangers and with it came a feeling among some of the media that this result would put a spoke in the Celtic wheel of progress that at that stage had seemed irreversible. But I was cautious about that given that Celtic had dominated much of the game and with perhaps a slice of luck might have won it. Somebody within Ibrox should have blessed the greatest Dane of them all now for giving the Rangers support a morale booster. But at the same time they should have enacted a ruthless self-examination of their status in the modern European game at a time when their manager was being criticised at that level and for too conservative an approach to football as opposed to what was occurring on the other side of the city. Well, they eventually did. But too late. And the rest, as they say, is history.

15

The Narrow Margin

Celtic v Rangers
1–0
Scottish League Cup Final
29 October 1966
Goal: Bobby Lennox

THE FRENCH WERE interested in this. Not because the Auld Alliance was being re-awakened. Their interest was very practical. The officials from a football club, that until then we hardly knew existed, were coming to Hampden to spy, quite openly on Celtic FC. Nantes FC had been drawn against Celtic in the next round of the European Cup after Celtic had eliminated Zurich FC in the first round. Of course, at that stage, creating interest among the public about a European tie, even amongst the club's own faithful, when we were on the verge of another Old Firm final would have been like a busker on the pavement trying to distract the customers away from the Palladium. Nothing could oust the visceral feeling of that old rivalry which had been intensified not only by the entry of Jock Stein into the scene, but that by the fact that after only seven months since taking over from the genial Jimmy McGrory he had beaten Rangers in the League Cup final in 1965, a game covered by my colleague George Davidson, as rookie me was at a league match at the same time. Over and above that, the League Cup had always been a difficult tournament for Celtic having only won it twice before that date.

Now I have heard it said more than once and not by the kind of folk who believe in the tooth fairy, that a good referee should be invisible; one who evokes the remark at the end of 90 minutes, 'Who was the referee?'

The referee that particular day in 1966 was as indiscernible as Mount Everest on a clear day. He was Tom 'Tiny' Wharton. Tiny was as broad as he was long. When he towered over the likes of wee Willie Henderson or 'Jinky' Johnstone it was like an act from a variety show that was about to burst into a comical song and dance act. Indeed, you often thought with such bulk Tiny's legs wouldn't make the full 90 minutes. And although that girth seemed to stamp him with an authority and respect that others couldn't achieve, many thought he refereed at long distance and didn't keep up with the play.

Years later, in an interview, I referred him to that afternoon and some of the hullabaloo associated with it. He played it lightly as if it was of such little significance, he could barely recall it. In truth I believe referees remember any controversies surrounding them as clearly as the birth of their first born.

Tiny certainly recalled a game that had two distinctive halves. Celtic had scored a goal in the 19th minute that put an entirely different complexion on the match. It was superb. Auld floated in a tantalising cross met by the head of McBride who headed it back into the penalty box where Bobby Lennox, sprinting like he had just come off his blocks, smashed it into the net. Now watching from the bench you had to wonder if Stein, identified as an attacking manager, would want to add to that. In fact that game suggested that it was more accurate to describe him as a pragmatist – a view a later game in Europe against Dukla Prague would seem to reinforce. For from then on Celtic were on the defensive and were outplayed by a Rangers side who simply had nobody menacing enough to capitalise on it despite their onslaught.

Enter Tiny. In the latter part of the first-half Bobby Watson scored what he thought was a legitimate equaliser. Tiny instead awarded a free kick to Celtic for what he considered a foul on Ronnie Simpson. Cue foaming at-the-mouth Rangers players who, enraged at that decision, conveniently forgot the astonishing misses they had already perpetrated and had to watch Willie O'Neil clear off the line near the end with Simpson well beaten, as a cruel postscript to their own aimless extravagance near goal. That goal-line save has been forgotten in the welter of stats connected with Celtic for initiating their historic campaign that season. Lennox's great goal has made us forget that a diligent full-back and an imperious referee played their part.

16

The Breakthrough

Celtic v Vojvodina Novi Sad
2–1
European Cup Quarter-Final
8 March 1967
Goal: Billy McNeill

THEY CHANGED THE commentary position at Celtic Park. During the McGrory era I worked on a platform from just in front of the main stand. It was not ideal since you couldn't attain the panoramic views that a stadium like that deserved. Some visionary decided to move it and into the covered enclosure on the opposite side we went. For the entire Stein era I commentated from above the 'Jungle', the denizens of which gave thunderous throat to the varying fortunes of the club, which under their new manager since March 1965, had risen in stock and heartened those who had feared remaining in the trough of mediocrity. Of all the times I held a microphone there and despite wearing headphones, I could clearly hear the sound rising from beneath me like a jury offering volcanic verdicts on performances on the field, with fearsome unanimity. The good or the bad registered on the eardrums as if they were of single voice harbouring no dissent. And of all the occasions when it was roused, nothing could possibly have exceeded the evening of 8 March 1967.

Celtic had reached the quarter-finals of the European Cup. As I recall, all the discussions that took place in the media from the start of that European campaign were appreciative of the club's efforts but, outside their own committed supporters, few thought they would go as far as this stage. This was their first venture at this exalted level of the game and with it came the usual self-doubts about the quality of the Scottish domestic game. Was it really good enough to produce a side that could go this far in such a widespread competition? But a handsome 3–1 victory over Nantes in France in the previous round in November had given many pause for serious thought. Could they really reach as far as the semi-finals? The first game against their quarter-final opponents Vojvodina lent scepticism to that idea. They were beaten 1–0 by the Slavs in the first leg. And indeed I recall Stevie Chalmers telling me once in no uncertain terms, years later, 'I think Vojvodina were the best team we played in the whole tournament!'

It's not that they were overwhelmed in Novi Sad in Serbia in the first leg. They only lost by a single goal and one that would cause unusual embarrassment to one of their most consistent players, Tommy Gemmell. Admittedly their defence was under constant pressure from the Slavs and in one single weak moment the Celtic full-back fluffed a pass-back to Ronnie Simpson in goal and a man called Stanić nipped in and scored the only goal of the game. Now I think what made that seem so worrying was the name Vojvodina itself. Hardly anybody knew anything about them outside Stein himself who would have known what their grannies had for breakfast in his normal preparatory investigations.

The general public, and not a few of us in the media, knew little about a side which didn't even come from Serbia's main city and given the illustrious names from Italian, Spanish and German football which people in the streets in Scotland could quote with ease, all this seemed like being beaten by yokels.

On the back of that, 69,734 came to Celtic Park that night to judge them and hope they were upstarts to be put down appropriately. On the platform in the Jungle you could feel the heat rising towards you like a corporate sweat was being generated through anxiety or just plain expectancy. Although they were there to give great vocal support to their team they were clearly unsure what to expect. As the game progressed I felt myself that their opponents were disciplined, organised, sensible and containing Celtic with a worrying ease for those sweating underneath me. Indeed, Pusibric should have scored in the fifth minute (scorning an easy chance). Had he scored the tie might have been beyond Celtic's reach. I look now at the time of the Celtic goal which came to equalise the aggregate score at 1–1. Fifty-eight minutes had gone when the keeper Pantelic had fumbled a cross by Gemmell and Chalmers poked it over the line. Like the denizens of the Jungle I felt it had been like an eternity.

It was a scrambled unspectacular goal but, like taking the cork out of a bottle, the loud pop from the Jungle indicated how vital it had been. But I was impressed by the highly technical Slavs who notably did not buckle under the thunderstorm of noise. Their competence was eating up the time after that goal. I could hear the growls of frustration mounting from below our platform. And from where I was I could see the Celtic dugout clearly, where Stein was looking more frequently at his watch. I had never seen him so agitated. According to what Sean Fallon was to tell me, Stein turned to him, with two minutes remaining and said in disgust, 'It looks like bloody Rotterdam!' Which is where the play-off would be. Then a corner was awarded to Celtic. Charlie Gallagher took it on the right into a highly congested penalty area. In the Jungle there seemed to be a communal holding of breath as the kick was taken.

Years later I was honoured to give the eulogy at Billy McNeill's funeral in Glasgow. I talked about his character, his personality and that memorable day in Lisbon eventually. I still regret I did not include that moment at Celtic Park when he strode into the penalty area, chest-out, determined, as hope was dwindling, against a defence which had handled similar corner kicks with ease. He rose, like we had watched him do in the game previously but with little effect. This time there was solid contact, with the ball rocketing into the roof of the net. Celtic were through. The Jungle's eruption shook our platform. They had won from a head which had served Celtic brilliantly but not with impunity. When I saw him in Glasgow's municipal building years later in the awful terminal stages of his dementia when he could not speak nor recognise me, you could not help but associate his great headed goal that night, and the many others in the past, to a process that was very possibly associated with his deterioration. If so, then it was not just a goal that sent them onwards that night, but also an act of self-sacrifice.

17

World Beaters

England v Scotland
2–3
Home International
15 April 1967
Goal: Jim McCalliog

HE WAS A young man who had never played professionally for a club in his native land. And now he was to face the world champions. At that stage Jim McCalliog was residing in Sheffield playing for Wednesday. It was obvious though that this exile could hardly be ignored when he was scoring a goal that would take that club into the FA Cup final against Everton. He also scored in that match to put his side 2–0 up but had to face a historic fightback by the Liverpool side which won 3–2. He was making his mark though. Making my way to Wembley I was aware I knew little about him, and probably would not have recognised him had I met him in the street. Which, despite his credence as a proven player in England, made me slightly circumspect about what I thought was perhaps a gamble. And certainly I was more interested in another striker. Denis Law was already a national icon. I had not yet shrugged off my adolescent adoration of the blonde striker and was obviously reluctant to do so. I desperately wanted him to score in this match more than anyone else whatever befell the Scottish side itself. Now he did score that day and anywhere I have gone in the world to talk about that goal and the significance of Scotland's win I am met with the rejoinder, 'Oh, you mean the keepy-uppy game?' That day bears a special identity that tends to overshadow the other events.

Jim Baxter had chosen to self-indulge in one of the most iconic settings in world football, Wembley stadium. As he played with the ball from foot to foot like he was in his back garden it was at a juncture when Scotland were well in the lead against the current World Champions England. It was as provocative as mooning the enemy before battle, as in days of yore, and with England still in contention in the match and players on the park like Nobby Stiles (who as we say in the trade, 'would kick his granny') I wondered if there would be unpleasant repercussions. Since it was still only 1–0, at that time, could it really have been the time for whetting the ribaldry of the strong anti-English sentiments crowding Wembley. Any time is the best time, I concluded, from the hearty response to his provocative playfulness.

It is true though that Scotland had been in comfortable control of this game with Baxter in languid, mesmerising form, backed up by the energetic and robust Billy Bremner. It was like hearing a fine violinist harmonising with the base drummer. This was a flowering of the fact that the Scots on the field were far from in awe of world champions.

Indeed, as the teams walked onto the pitch listening to the full-throated 30,000 Scots, sounding like the majority, you could tell they were clearly unaffected by England's special status, as if all they had done was to win a Millport summer five-a-side tournament. Indeed, I was surprised at just how confident the Scots folk were, even though it had been drummed into them by the English media that their current side under Alf Ramsey hadn't lost a match in two whole years. It occurred to me that to our optimistic supporters, England were seen as that ruffian biblical giant who was just asking for a spectacular downfall.

So who would be our David? No great surprise when Denis Law stepped into that frame almost on the half-hour to take a rebound off the keeper and drive it home to put Scotland 1–0 in the lead. It didn't quite make my day but it was well on the way to doing so. By this time I was assessing McCalliog for the first time. He seemed to be quite at home amongst this exalted company. Now in the background in club football Celtic were leading 3–1 from the home leg against Dukla Prague in the semi-final of the European Cup and looked highly likely to reach the final itself. And in the pre-match interviews I sensed even from English journalists a curiosity about that achievement. It was almost as if it were freakish and didn't really represent the true nature of Scottish football which they felt was merely useful for exporting outstanding individuals and that our chronic problem was fitting them properly into a national side. So that is why the selection of Bobby Lennox was compellingly interesting. In the first place he was to admit to me in a long interview I did with him looking back over his career that he was proud of the ten times he had played for Scotland but like many in the Celtic fraternity believed that more caps should have gone to Celtic players through the years. Said without bitterness, and almost melancholically.

So I found I was drifting away from my Law obsession and concentrating on the two newcomers. They both looked to the manner born. And what magnified their achievements was that they were compressed into the last 12 minutes of the game. The first to open the throats of the support was Bobby Lennox. Previously, the English, aware of his speed had contained him well. But in a quick flurry of attacking and the English not clearing their lines cleanly the winger with just a brief look at the ball at his feet swept it into the net with his right foot from just inside the penalty area. It may not have occurred to him at the time or thereafter, but he had become the first Celtic player ever to score at Wembley. 2–0. Then just after the limping Jack Charlton had pulled one back at 2–1 came the goal that I recall most of all. The youngest player on the field, the exile, the gamble, enlightened us to his quick feet. McCalliog's slick give-and-go in tight space before he struck, oozed of maturity. It was an achievement because it overshadowed the Law goal for me and I said so in my summary, almost feeling guilty about turning my back on my hero.

But, if you had to judge by the chat in the Wembley bars among the media, it was the Baxter sideshow they were talking about mainly, particularly among the English journalists who, stung by the result, wanted some kind of diversion from their obvious discomfort. For the first time in decades though you could feel the eyes of the world were on us. Although, losing 2–0 to the USSR at Hampden in a friendly only four weeks later reminded the world and ourselves that 'keepy-uppy' games were rarities that were about self-indulgence, not progress.

18

Guid Gear

Rangers v Celtic
6 May 1967
2–2
Goal: Jimmy Johnstone

WHEN I WAS in school-teaching in Lanarkshire I heard about a boy called Johnstone who was so skilled on a football field that the teacher who ran the St Columba's school-team, a man called Crines, had kept him on until he was almost 14 before allowing him to be transferred to his secondary school. I lost track of him for a considerable time until I heard the name Jimmy Johnstone being announced in the Celtic team selection for the Scottish Cup final on 4 May 1963, the first Old Firm final in 25 years and only a year after I had started broadcasting. Could that actually be the same boy I had heard about not all that long ago? It was. In a dreich day of unrelenting rain, his diminutive form, topped in the gloom by almost incandescent red-hair pranced impishly on the sodden surface. Peter Wilson of the *Daily Mirror* wrote of his performance, '...he chased the ball in the manner reminiscent of Harpo Marx chasing blondes in his palmy days'.

To little effect, because the rest of the Celtic team were below par and fortunate to survive to a replay which Rangers won with ease 3–0, with the little red-head having been dropped. So as I approached Ibrox on 6 May 1967 the weather reminded me of that cup final day four years earlier with the rain relentless, but the football circumstances completely transformed. For Celtic were now a power in the land having won the Scottish Cup on the previous Saturday and only needed to avoid defeat against Rangers that day to win the league title. On top of that, exactly three weeks later they were to play Inter Milan in the European Cup final having powered to a commanding position in European football under the relatively short reign of Jock Stein.

Rangers were floundering by comparison but could have thwarted Celtic's ambitions that soggy day. But Johnstone was no longer just an entertaining but feckless performer. He was now 'Jinky' having grown in affection with the Celtic support for his valued contributions to Stein's master plans. As I walked to the stadium I observed a man who was there to make a professional evaluation of Celtic before the European final. Helenio Herrera the manager of Inter. He was a small, inoffensive-looking individual with a gigantic reputation for having won league titles in both Spain and Italy. He had his eyes opened that day by a man even smaller than himself. For 'Jinky' was no longer 'chasing blondes' he was an integral part of a side whose basic nature was to be on the offensive. Although Rangers opened the scoring just before half-time, 'Jinky' sneaked in behind a group of players to toe-poke an equaliser only a single minute later. It is what happened in the 74th minute that must have had Herrera scribbling furiously in his notebook.

Picking up a pass on the touchline, 'Jinky' made the now historic decision to cut inside the Rangers defence instead of moving wide down the right. Nevertheless, even though at pace it did not look imminently dangerous, particularly as the ball was on his left side, suddenly he let fly from 25 yards out. There was barely a deviation in its trajectory as the ball beat Martin in goal by pace and accuracy and he could only look above himself eventually to see it nestling in the top corner of the net. 2–1. Many of Jinky's colleagues must themselves have been astonished by how such a little man could have used his so-called weaker left foot to achieve that power with such a heavy ball.

I am emboldened to say that he could not have scored a greater goal in all his career. Yes, Rangers did eventually equalise for the game to end 2–2. But the wee man had effectively won a title for Celtic. Helenio Herrera left Ibrox having learned the meaning of that old Scottish expression 'Guid gear comes in sma' bulk!'

19

The Peak

Celtic v Inter Milan
2–1
25 May 1967
Goal: Stevie Chalmers

'Jock Stein et Helenio Herrera faillerent en venir au mains'

The footballing world and even those outside it who loved a fleshy human story, were captivated that day in May by the events in Lisbon. For example, the quote above comes from a highly respected French magazine and roughly translated means that the two managers almost came to blows in the tunnel at half-time in the game. Yes, I did hear about that in the stadium later that day when I was still trying to come to terms with how lucky I actually was to be there at all. At that stage in life I was a headmaster of a school in Lanarkshire, working part-time for the BBC. The office in Glasgow was keen to have a Scottish voice at the game, one way or the other, so asked me if I could go and share with the English commentator, Kenneth Wolstenholme. I sent a request to the Director of Education John S McEwan, for leave of absence for three days, who not surprisingly rejected it. Not to be outdone, I tried another approach. The local MP was Jimmy Hamilton, who occasionally visited my school because of his interest in education. Now when I had been commentating at Celtic Park I couldn't have failed to notice the same man enjoying hospitality at every game in the director's box, as a devoted follower. So I contacted him and explained the situation to him. When he uttered the well-known politician's phrase, 'Leave it to me,' I didn't hold out much hope. But, lo and behold, a day later came a call from the education office giving me permission to be released, if I could find a replacement. I did. My wife. A qualified teacher herself. So as I walked into the Celtic training camp the day before that game still in something of a dream I had to thank an MP, and a wife for getting me there.

And admittedly I did feel like an intruder at first, that I was not like the full-time professional which Wolstenholme certainly was. But, he certainly soaked in what I had to inform him about Celtic as he was not as clued up as I thought he might have been. I sat with him in a café for hours going back as far as relating how four years previously Jock Stein along with his great adversary Willie Waddell, who was managing Kilmarnock at the time, travelled to Milan to learn something about the methods and thinking of Helenio Herrera the Inter manager who was influencing football throughout the continent and in which tenure he would win three Serie A titles and two European Cups.

For he was the architect of the *catenaccio* system which could have inspired the builders of the Berlin Wall, so structurally defensive it was. Now Stein was impressed by his thoroughness in the way he prepared his players for games but looked upon Herrera's basic negative structure, no matter how successful it appeared to be, the way a vegetarian would look upon a rump steak. To say the least, it was not to his taste and we were all witnesses to the collision of values that day.

The setting was perfect. The skies were incandescently blue. The stadium had the appearance of a community focal point rather than just a football arena, cosy in a kind of way. The heat was for shirt-sleeves. The Inter jerseys looked gloomy and menacing compared to Celtic's gear. A highly visible contrast to start with. So was the football to be. At first I couldn't discern any particular pattern but then we were jolted by one significant incident. For nobody after it could have been optimistic about attacking instincts surviving the afternoon when after only eight minutes Jim Craig tackled Cappellini in the box and a penalty was awarded. Stein in his white-shirted seat on the bench in the glorious sunshine, looked upon Cappellini's reaction as belonging to the artificial death throes of a singer in Italian Grand Opera. So at half-time walking back in the tunnel he did address that thought to Herrera as fists were ominously raised, as well as calling the German referee Tschenscher a 'Nazi' for manipulating it for the Italians.

That fury was to pass and I can remember that second-half as a celebration of the positive properties of sport, of a triumph of the master of optimism against the peddler of the dark arts. Celtic were ceaseless in their momentum towards the Inter goal with possession of the ball that made the Italians look secure to us, but with a monotony that, unattractive as it looked, nevertheless looked composed and self-confident. That is why to Kenneth Wolstenholme and myself in the commentary box, the Tommy Gemmell equaliser in the 62nd minute was like a whiff of oxygen in an increasingly suffocating atmosphere of continuing Celtic attacks with nothing to show for them. The way he struck it from just outside the box to bulge the net was like an exclamation of rejection of the way Inter were playing, not merely a goal. It utterly changed the mood. You could sense that Inter were affected in a way that made you think they were not only shocked but that they were actually beginning to look weary. Tommy was to tell me weeks later, 'An Italian defender comes out to meet me. But then he stops about two yards from me and turns his back. If he had kept coming and kept facing me I would never have got that shot in and the whole history of the Lions would have been changed.' Hindsight can sometimes produce undue modesty!

That moment is simply imperishable in recollection because of its spectacular design. Yes, the winner itself made special history when Stevie Chalmers, five minutes from the end cunningly invaded the penalty box and screwed the ball away from Sarti in goal for the 2–1 winner. It seemed a trifle mundane compared to the Gemmell flourish if you examined it clinically outside the circumstances. But, of course, nobody ever has. It brought a special cup back to UK shores for the first time.

The Portuguese television producer on the spot asked me if I would go to the PA mike and address the Celtic fans who were now in their thousands carousing on the pitch, and ask them if they would clear the pitch so the presentation could take place. So I did. They were deafened by jubilation and moved not an inch. However, what it meant was that the Celtic captain had to make his weary way around the outside of the stadium to get to the presentation area just in front of our commentary position where I could clearly see a man who had given his all and was on his last legs. The sudden rejuvenation came with the lifting of the cup itself.

Celtic were now European Champions, and on the spot I thought of how Stein had walked into Celtic Park that March day only just over two short years previously, and found it difficult to absorb what I had just witnessed. But I was fortunate to be a witness at all, of course. I knew part-time with the BBC was no longer viable. I returned to Glasgow with a resolution on the back of that triumph which had altered my view on life. Shortly after, when the opportunity came along, I joined the Corporation full-time and years later thanked Stevie Chalmers for helping to change my career. I doubt if he ever thought that was his greatest triumph.

20

Granite Approach

Celtic v Aberdeen
1–3
Scottish Cup Final
11 April 1970
Goal: Joe Harper

EDDIE TURNBULL HAD the saltiest tongue of them all, in my experience. I came to know him well as a manager who could use words to great stunning effect. My first face-to-face with him was when he was Aberdeen manager only a few days away from playing Jock Stein's Celtic in that cup final. My initial respect for Ned (as Turnbull was referred to by friend or foe) stemmed from his reputation for having played for Hibernian as one of the Famous Five, which evoked the universal respect you might harbour for veterans of El Alamein. During that morning interview at Pittodrie a joiner, interrupting the recording by his hammering in the stand, was treated to the kind of verbal profane blasting from Ned that made the man cringe like he was under rifle fire. On 5 August 1972 Hibs, managed by Ned, trounced Celtic 5–3, after extra-time at Hampden in the Drybrough Cup final, that commercial tournament which preceded the league season. It was something of a shock. So after the game I went to the dressing room door behind which I could hear the Hibs celebrations shaking the stand. He opened it himself and agreed to come out for an interview. We waited patiently for half an hour for him and then wired him up for the interview. I was about to deliver my first question when he suddenly asked, 'How much am I getting for this?' I had to tell him that off the top of the head I could not say. To which he replied, 'Well, f--- off then,' ripped off his mike and stormed off.

For throughout his career Eddie Turnbull evoked analogies with other personalities when you attempted to define his own, like Genghis Khan, for example. It all depended to whom you talked, or from your own experience of a man not only with a volatile temperament, that in its volcanic form could strip paint off walls and was sometimes laced with curses. I write this not of a man I disliked. I really warmed to him because he was blunt, crude at times, but totally open.

Stein, who himself could repel a Sherman tank when in the mood, but with a great deal more cunning in his make-up, really respected him though. They had played against each other in the Coronation Cup final of 20 May 1953 which Celtic won and helped boost the career of the man from Burnbank. I saw Ned play only once. When I was a boy and on holiday in Dunoon, 'doon the watter' my father took me on the ferry to Greenock to watch Hibs play Morton. It was a day when the rain, not untypically for the region, was coming down like stair-rods and the notorious Cappielow pitch looked like chocolate pudding to me. My father was not interested in Turnbull, he was there to see Gordon Smith, Hibs right-winger who was getting rave reviews for his elegant play. Sadly, he was rarely seen on that muddy surface which clearly was totally unsuited to his style of play. Turnbull though I still recall after all this time taking shots at goal, one of which cannoned off the crossbar and reverberated for us behind the goal, semaphoring the message that this was one tough competitor.

So in Ned's interview with me at Pittodrie that day when I brought up the subject of that Coronation Cup final, he notably bridled, as if I were trying to rile him and you could tell the mood was suffused with the notion of revenge. Another name though was to cling to this Scottish Cup final for years, RH Davidson. A referee from Airdrie. Perhaps, THE referee when it came to dealing with controversy. He never looked to be affected by such, and in a strange way you felt he might have sought after it. He awarded a penalty to Aberdeen in the 27th minute for what he considered deliberate handling in the box by Bobby Murdoch. Deliberate? Tommy Gemmell was so incensed by the award he threw the ball at Davidson and was booked for an offence that would have been red-carded in later years.

At half-time Stein's voice could have been heard castigating Davidson as far away as Airdrie itself. Protestation had made no difference. Joe Harper like a man insulated from any provocation had sent the keeper

Evan Williams the wrong way from the spot. 1–0 half-time. That coolness was impressive. As was Aberdeen's measured, stubborn, triumphant defence of their lead and indeed adding to it through two Derek McKay late goals, particularly his second coming virtually on the final whistle after Celtic's Bobby Lennox had pulled one back. 3–1 it was.

But it is the Harper penalty that was so significant and the impassive resilience of referee Davidson to insist his decision was correct. He was to be pursued for the rest of his career by Stein, who followed him, rather like the posse who pursued Butch Cassidy and the Sundance Kid, with critical comments whenever he could. Although that day Stein recognised the worth of Aberdeen's achievement by personally delivering champagne to the winners' dressing room afterwards. Ned's reputation soared. Because he had beaten a master who had taken on a final between the two European Cup semi-finals against Leeds and was a measure of the level Aberdeen had to attain for a win. The only other time the Dons had won the trophy was much earlier in 1947 when one of their opponents was a Hibs player named Eddie Turnbull.

21

Full House

Celtic v Leeds
2–1
European Cup Semi-Final (second leg)
15 April 1970
Goal: Bobby Murdoch

THE FIRST THING that was broken that night was a record. From my position in the press-box you could tell the crowd was extraordinary. In fact, it still remains a European Cup Champions League record of 136,505, as we learned later – comprising of virtually all Celtic devotees, as tickets had been returned from Leeds the day before, obviously on the basis of that club's defeat in the first leg 1–0 at Elland Road. But, of course, Celtic would be facing players accustomed not only to enduring hostility around grounds in England, but having to cope with an English media which occasionally treated them like Northerners of a distinctly provincial character. This was clear to me at the press conference just after Leeds had arrived in Glasgow. They did not seem particularly warm when questioning Don Revie the Leeds manager. Later when they became more loose-tongued having some drinks with me they regarded Revie as some kind of lonesome, chilly, football pedant whom they simply did not trust, quite regardless of his immense record with Leeds in both domestic and European football. I did get the feeling though that if Revie had planked himself down with Arsenal or Spurs in London they might have had more time for him. I would go far as to say that some of them would be quietly rejoicing if he were to flounder at Hampden. Interestingly, given that they had sampled the mastery of Jock Stein's winning tactics in the first game, even then they were talking about how he would fare in English football if ever he came that way. It is the only game I ever approached learning that a visiting team to Glasgow lacked proper sympathy from much of their own media.

Years later Bertie Auld told me of Stein's team-talk before the game, and of how the English media were not wildly off the mark. 'Revie's shittin' himself,' he told them. 'I've never seen that man as nervous in all my life. He's as white as a sheet. What do you think his players are like? They are there for the taking, believe you me.'

In a preview I called it a surrogate European final, because on the face of it they were the two most renowned teams left in the competition, or so we thought at the time. Celtic, and the volume of the surrounding terracing blast, were in a superior collaboration from the very outset. Six corners forced in the first eight minutes, no less. Leeds looked strangely ill-equipped. Then came an abrupt awakening. It was after intense Celtic attacking amidst thunderous noise from their huge support. In 14 minutes Billy Bremner produced a 25 yard rocket which went into the net off the junction of post and crossbar to put Leeds one up. As spectacular a goal as Hampden had seen in ages. It was as if someone had screamed, 'Weel done Cutty Sark... and in an instant all was dark'. Because it utterly silenced Hampden and my immediate thought was 'The cunning Revie has worked this all out.'

He hadn't. In such circumstances an equaliser would instantly reinstate Celtic as the superior side, which they were. That's why when it came and from which player, made it the most significant goal of the game for me. John Hughes had a career-lasting tempestuous relationship with Stein. So much so that the player stated publicly years later, that it would have been hypocrisy had he attended his former manager's funeral. Which is why I vividly recall Hughes' celebration when he put his head to an Auld cross, from a short Davy Hay corner, to equalise at a perfect juncture for a positive Celtic rebound, two minutes into the second-half. He was like a man who had proved some kind of point, or perhaps even telling the crowd he really should have been a Lisbon Lion as well, but couldn't because of injury at that time.

There was only one winning team after that. The second goal, four minutes after the Hughes strike, a stunning smash by Bobby Murdoch after a one-two with Jinky who had been running the Leeds defence ragged for the second game in a row, put Celtic into their second European Cup final. Murdoch was a mix of strength and conviction. Game after game he would provide the substance to the side with accurate passing and tigerish tackles. Sometimes when you watched a player like that you felt his own side and people who followed the club constantly would appreciate his worth, but perhaps not the general public. That striking goal was his dramatic way of introducing himself to a totally British and European audience. As a consequence we could hardly avoid making comparisons with how Celtic would prepare for this coming final in the San Siro in Milan with that for Lisbon three years before. To many of us it was to be like comparing a stagecoach to the Royal Scot.

22

The Miscalculation

Celtic v Feyenoord
1–2
European Cup Final
Milan, 6 May 1970
Goal: Tommy Gemmell

COMPLACENCY CAN SPREAD virally in football. Viewing the prospect of the approaching final between Celtic, who had won the European Cup three years previously, and the Dutch club Feyenoord, who had only become professional 13 years before, did not seem to require profound analysis. After all Celtic had disposed of a major threat in Leeds, managed by one of the shrewdest brains in European football and had become 3–1 on favourites to lift the trophy. So we settled inevitably into a comfortable acquiescence with the bookies foresight. Like others I would forecast a Celtic win with less apprehension than in previous times because of the quality of their victory in the semi-final. However, the general mood among the media trying to evaluate this fixture and put some credence on the Dutch challenge, was being affected by the master himself.

Jock Stein was a different man from the figure who went to Lisbon in dynamic mood and as if his very life was at stake. His attention to detail in preparation bordered on fanaticism. For example, one day in the hotel before that '67 final I was sitting talking to his reserve goalkeeper John Fallon in a lounge with the sun striking his head through the window. Stein pounced on us and blasted his keeper for not realising the sun sapped energy. And Fallon was never likely to play in that final anyway.

The change of approach before the Milan final was in stark display in their training camp in the hills of Varese north of Milan. Players and press mingled, chatted, joshed around and even surreptitiously had a drink or two. To those of us who had been in Lisbon it was bewildering. And Tommy Gemmell was to tell me years after, 'I didn't agree with his team selection. And as for his team-talk it was so downbeat that you would have thought we were going out to play Partick Thistle'. Stein was manifestly relaxed in his interviews and so were the media. We had all been infected. Yes, the Dutch side Ajax had reached the final the year previously to offer us an indication of the improvement in that nation's football. But they had been thrashed by AC Milan in the final 4–1. That in itself took care of any more detailed analysis of Dutch football it seemed.

So the first sight of the red and white jerseys of Feyenoord in the San Siro that night did not set my pulse racing. Stein had watched them in domestic action and returned unimpressed, describing one of their so-called star players Wim Van Hanegem as a 'slower Jim Baxter with a right foot just for standing on.' Bobby Lennox was to tell me that the Dutchman was actually superb and nobody could get near him. Stein also told his players of the man who was to become a future Celtic manager, Wim Jansen, that he could only play for 20 minutes before disappearing. When Bertie Auld was manager of Partick Thistle in the future, he and I would sit in his office after some games at Firhill as he reflected on some of the significant moments of his past under Stein. He brought up that assessment of Jansen to me facetiously. 'Jock was right enough about that. I never did see Jansen after that. He got faster as we seemed to get slower. He was just too good for me.'

I think it was about 20 minutes into the game when I realised I was watching something different from the Dutch. Simply put, it was possession football. Celtic were finding it difficult to take the ball from them, with their neat inter-passing and watching Van Hanegem nutmeg Bobby Lennox with that left foot on one occasion suggested that same player had conned the spying Celtic manager for the first time in his life. Up front the mobile, talented spearhead Ove Kindvall was dragging Billy McNeill in all directions and creating gaps. The Dutch to our chagrin were in total command.

Which is why the Tommy Gemmell goal on 30 minutes seemed like a dramatic reminder that Celtic had not actually missed the flight to Milan. The low free kick finding the net to make it 1–0 had the obvious promise of the man, who also scored in Lisbon, leading a revival, and also suggesting the Dutch were only masters of possession but minus the real menace Celtic had in their ranks. However, the Dutch equaliser only two minutes later when the Feyenoord captain Israel took advantage of almost amateurish defending by Celtic to level the score, you could say brought us to our senses and to accept that Feyenoord were out-classing their opponents. That it had to take them until four minutes to the end of extra-time to score the winner – a delightful lob by Kindvall over Williams in goal, after McNeill had totally misjudged a free kick from the half-way line – was one of the two major puzzles of the night. The other was how John Hughes missed a chance in front of goal, in extra-time, that I thought a schoolboy would have scored, instead hitting the keeper with the ball and causing him to say in later years, '…when I did that, that was me finished at Celtic.'

However, the Gemmell goal remains poignant to me especially if you link it to his words above. For a man who went into a game with obvious dubiety about team selection, among other doubts, his strike could not have signalled devotion to his leader any more dramatically.

But he was also painfully aware that the commanding figure who had brought back that cup for the first time to British shores had not only failed to regain it and enhance his club's reputation in Europe but had done so because of a brutal truth, as expressed to me by Tommy Gemmell, Jock Stein had lost the plot.

23

Teenage Debut

Rangers v Celtic
Scottish League Cup Final
24 October 1970
1–0
Goal: Derek Johnstone

'IF MY WIFE had got her hands on you on Saturday night, she would have torn your eyes out!' So said the former manager of Rangers Scot Symon when I had accidentally come across him in the Isle of Skye hotel in Perth a week after he had been sacked by the club in November 1967. He was referring to his domestic reaction to an interview I had conducted on the previous Saturday edition of *Sportscene*. I had invited into the studio a man highly respected in the game even by his sternest opponents. Ian McMillan, an inside-forward of subtle skills, was christened the 'Wee Prime Minister' after his namesake Harold, not only because he was universally acknowledged as a dominant figure in the game but because of his gentlemanly demeanour about which, it was said, the worst expletive he ever uttered on the field was, 'Away and pee!' Thus, he had the kind of respect I needed to talk honestly about Symon.

He did. Effectively. In very polite soft tones. He told of the time they played Eintracht Frankfurt in the semi-final of the European Cup, and after being given the runaround by a much better team in the first half, at half-time with the score 1–1 the structure needed to change. According to McMillan Symon hardly spoke and sat in a corner of the dressing room sipping a cup of tea instead. It was a silent assassination by McMillan. Hence the rise in blood pressure within a certain household.

There was less anger outside that suburban dwelling where the Rangers support were witnessing a powerful new figure beginning to threaten the staid and conventional management of Rangers who had been astonishingly dumped out of the Scottish Cup on 28 January 1967 by lowly Berwick Rangers. This at a time when Jock Stein was demanding attention. Although Symon's exit could have been handled with more decorum when Rangers were in fact at the top of the league at that juncture, the general feeling was that his time was up. The man they chose to replace him was an articulate modernist David White but with no clout in his make-up and he left in a couple of years later as the first Rangers manager never to win a trophy.

They turned to a journalist who had Ibrox written all over him. Willie Waddell, a former Rangers player of renown and formidable personality who had won the league title as manager of Kilmarnock. He was appointed to Ibrox in late 1969 and when he was to clash with Stein for the first time as manager in a cup final on 24 October 1970 for the League Cup, I recall the mood among the media was as if they were writing about a heavyweight fight about to take place at Madison Square Garden. All the mood music was Wagnerian. For one or another it was to be Doomsday given the stature of the two men in charge.

Firstly, came the puzzle of the Rangers team selection. We had known in advance they were going to be severely handicapped by the absence of flu victim, captain John Greig who was such an influence in the side that it was like hearing of a modern car losing its satnav. In fact, I could not see how they could possibly fill that vacuum to effect which made my clear-cut prediction of a Celtic win. Then the team sheet was handed to me about half an hour before the game and I noted the name Derek Johnstone there. Who was he? Now it may well have been because I was not keeping up with developments at Ibrox at the time, amongst their youth, but I certainly had never heard of him, not even in a whisper. And I recall the flutter in the Hampden press-box an hour before kick-off as many a journalist was now on the phone trying to glean some information on a lad whom we believed only to be 16 years of age. That dominated my introduction as the teams ran out with our cameras and the eyes of the media trained on one particular individual. Johnstone on first impression did not seem to be 16. He was tall and well-built and certainly in his first few touches seemed to be suffering no stage fright. Still, a lad that young making his debut in a cup final? It did not seem a feasible proposition. And yet Rangers were decidedly the better side in that first-half and Evan Williams in the Celtic goal had to make a series of saves that reflected the nature of the game accurately on a pitch that had been affected by the heavy rain. It was giving me pause for thought even with a mike to my mouth.

In fact the separation between winning and losing was by a single goal, which was almost absurdly orthodox in its execution. But it was with such conviction and with a look of maturity that the moment has almost been immortalised by the Ibrox faithful. Five minutes from half-time with little evidence of impending superiority, a long ball found the left-sided Willie Johnston popping up near the right corner flag and with his right foot he swept a high lob to near the penalty spot. The sort of cross that normally the Celtic captain Billy McNeill could actually yawn and deal with. However, the 16-year-old, precise with his leap, beat him to it and with a little flick of the left side of his head glided the ball past Evan Williams in goal. Even veteran press-men close to me were stunned. Ok, but there's a long way to go in the game. A 16-year-old winning a cup for Rangers? Impossible. I sensed that clearly. That was it though. One goal out of the textbook from a boy who had probably not yet thrown off the full effects of puberty.

In his interview with me afterwards the Rangers manager was a model of restraint. He was clearly overjoyed that his gamble had spectacularly paid off. He was never a man to wax lyrical. Not only had that boy won a cup for him, but the daring achievement would have bolstered his credibility amongst the Ibrox support. For any reverse for Celtic, who might have been falling short in recent times but were still mounting up league flags, was therapy for Ibrox. In a sense Derek Johnstone has never aged for many who were there to witness his achievement. He remains that teenager in the mind's eye to them, with a memory that for that generation is like an undying tonic. It was also now the third cup final Celtic had lost in 1970 – to Aberdeen, Feyenoord and now their great rivals. Leaving you to ponder which of the three was the most painful.

24

How to Burst a Coupon

Partick Thistle v Celtic
4–1
Scottish League Cup Final
23 October 1971
Goal: Denis McQuade

THE DAY BEFORE this final Sam Leitch, the heavyweight presenter of *Football Focus* on *Grandstand*, and whose authoritative pronouncements were taken as gospel throughout the UK, phoned me, as he occasionally did, for current Scottish football info and gossip, and asked me what I thought of Partick Thistle's chances against Celtic. 'Nae chance. None whatsoever,' I told him glibly. The following day to his massive audience he announced, 'In Scotland it's League Cup final day at Hampden Park where Celtic meet Partick Thistle, who have little chance.' The following week, post-final, I received a card from him with a multi-coloured clown with a tear rolling down his cheek and inside two words, only, 'Thanks, mate.' And underneath the score of that final. 4–1. These two words were so weighed down with sarcasm I thought the card must have been delivered by a two-ton lorry. Of course, I could also have sent him a script especially written for the information of the English audience, some of which would have gone like this, 'This is Partick Thistle we are talking about. The Great Unpredictables. The Maryhill Magyars. One day up, another day down. Known to break coupons with the flourish of bank robbers. Loved by their fans for being not Old Firm and regard the "lums" reeking around Maryhill as signs to civilisation that they are to be ignored at anybody's peril.' I could also have added Billy Connolly's assessment of Thistle's history, 'I grew up thinking they were called Partick Thistle Nil'. That would have been too much for them.

Thistle were an endearment to many in the game for as long as I can recollect, in their time in the top echelon. They decorated it with an almost charming inconsistency, beloved even by some of their loyalists, who like any others did like a win, but on the other hand relished the notion that their club occupied a special niche in Scottish football where they could be seen to have foresworn winning trophies for the role of adorable supporting actors. Yes, they had won the Scottish Cup in 1921 beating Rangers 1–0, at Celtic Park no less. But since then most clubs felt there was little threat coming from Maryhill in Glasgow, but, in making up the numbers were useful to have around, like the Salvation Army. So now they were up against the mighty Jock Stein who had rocked all of Europe only four years before and fielded that day a strong side, although minus the inspirational figure of the injured Billy McNeill. That did not seem so significant to the media who honestly felt Celtic could have fielded their groundsman in his place and still triumphed.

In the commentator's seat I felt like I was sitting back waiting for the Celtic deluge. What I then went through was one of the strangest experiences of all with a mike. I admit though that it is difficult to recall when the slightest smidgeon of doubt about Celtic's assumed supremacy began to surface. Yes, when Alex Rae scored with a beautifully lobbed goal over a crowded penalty area in ten minutes it was simply noted without too much fuss, because these sorts of free-wheeling moments happen in cup finals. I reflected that in my words to the public. In short I was preparing the audience for a vicious Celtic reaction. Then when Alex Lawrie swept in a right-footed low drive from the right-side of the penalty area to make it 2–0 I was more erect in my seat but hardly dismissive of Celtic's renowned fighting spirit. It would come.

And then came an incident that I completely underrated. Jimmy Johnstone was injured in a tackle and had to go off. But he was replaced by defender Jim Craig. Astonishingly Celtic did not have an appropriate forward on the bench. In the inquest afterwards it would be brought up as to how Jock Stein might have totally misjudged the occasion. Still, there on the spot I felt there was still a long way to go. So when did I stop ruminating about a Celtic fightback and grasp what was happening before my very eyes? There is no doubt about that.

It was the Denis McQuade third goal from close range in 28 minutes which tipped me into woozy incredulity, coping with the contemplation of a Celtic defeat. That goal itself summarised Celtic's afternoon. Unable to clear a corner properly allowed McQuade, to his own surprise, to score from close-in. Simple but with significance. For I always felt about games that the difference between a two-goal and three-goal deficit was like the difference between a bridgeable gap and a chasm. It was now like the feeling you get watching a foreign language film without subtitles, where it is obvious what is happening in front of your eyes but it is still largely incomprehensible. I had to switch commentary tone. This was not just about trying to explain the action. This was about trying to explain the almost inexplicable; that Celtic were being made to look like defensive novices in a cup final!

And as for the next goal, Jimmy Bone uncovered and almost walked the ball into the net for 4–0 shortly before half-time. That led to the craziest half-time interval I have ever experienced. I left my position and walked around the press-box almost as if I needed to verify whether I still had my senses intact. It was acoustical mayhem. The voices clattering against one another, like their disbelief was a thick undergrowth out of which they would have to emerge with a reasonable explanation for it all. For it was all over. Yes, Celtic's Kenny Dalglish did score 20 minutes from the end but only to record 4–1 for the history books.

The world did not shift on its axis, for orthodoxy took over again with Celtic heading for other triumphs and Thistle re-adopting their role as purveyors of the unpredictable. And, as near as dammit, Scottish football now had on record its equivalent of the sinking of the Titanic.

25

One Crowded Spanish Evening

Rangers v Dynamo Moscow
3–2
European Cup Winners' Cup Final
24 May 1972
Goal: Willie Johnston

AT FIRST IT seemed like a holiday break in the sun. In fact, the media were booked into the same pre-match hotel as the players in Castelldefels just down the coast from Barcelona, and we would share the breakfast tables with them like we were one big happy family. I recall that one of the favourite chats in the morning was all of us trying to find out who had the mystery room. We had been told by the chattering receptionist on arrival that the famous Hollywood actor George Sanders had committed suicide, only the month before, in one of the rooms and although we wanted to draw lots amongst the entire group to get possession of it, and indulge in idle boasting thereafter, it was never divulged. Anyway, after experiencing their room service we began to believe he might have died of malnutrition.

All this was the product of the nervous systems trying to avoid contemplating what might happen in the Camp Nou on the 24th. I admit I knew little about Rangers' opponents Dynamo. Russia in the '70s had become Stalinist again under Brezhnev, and I was told it was too awkward for me to travel to preview them, or BBC Scotland was going through a stingy period, or perhaps a bit of both. It didn't happen anyway. However, not seeing them in the flesh beforehand didn't seem to bother me all that much, because the city of Barcelona itself, and its long adjacent spectacular coastline, induced an 'It'll-be-all-right-on-the-night,' feeling for my broadcast. Straightforward. Nae bother. Twenty minutes from the end of the match itself with a Rangers supporter trying to force himself onto my knee and offering me a slug of Fundador straight from his bottle, even though my mike was to mouth, I knew I could no longer boast about my instinctive ability to prepare for any eventuality.

But, long before that incident, and well before the match itself, there were distinct signs that this was going to be no ordinary event. Earlier in the match-day, many hours before kick-off, we ambled to the magnificent Grand Canyon of football, the Camp Nou to try to familiarise ourselves with its initial intimidatory feel. We were surprised on two counts. Firstly, the field was covered by Rangers supporters; men, women and children bedecked in red, white and blue and looking like they had taken possession of the green sward with the few police who were there offering no strictures about the sanctity of the pitch and actually posing for photos with the Scots. Had Franco's fearsome robotic Guardia Civil now become benevolent tour guides? It struck me simply as odd. Then I was shown my commentary position which normally should have been up top, near the rim of the stadium. That night it was to be low down, near the touchline. That was going to be vital in my recollection of ensuing events.

And the goals that I commentated on eventually? Because of what was to explode in all our faces after the match, I have always looked back at them as if I am trying to distinguish figures in a snowstorm. Or when I am asked about the football that took place it's like I am being asked what the orchestra was playing when that iceberg hit the Titanic. But I do now realise that the goals had an effect that would have long-lasting consequences for Rangers, for Scottish football, and for one man in particular.

The first goal came in 24 minutes after Rangers looked to have adjusted comfortably to the fact that they were playing without their regular centre-half Colin Jackson, who forlornly sat it out on the bench, with striker Derek Johnstone taking his place but looking comfortable in a position to which he was certainly not unaccustomed. The Russians looked as if they had not yet emerged from their long winter and looked stiff and almost overwhelmed by the occasion. Dave Smith, in midfield and against men who were not as spritely as they had anticipated, was streaming out passes to great effect. One of them in 24 minutes found the foraging, striding Colin Stein who swept Rangers into the lead. 1–0. Smith again with a chip across goal found the head of Willie Johnston to head in the second five minutes from half-time. 2–0. And as I can recall at that stage I was being recognised by Rangers fans in my near-the-touchline position. Naturally they were being exuberant and were clearly intent on getting some of their comments on the air. I ploughed on with the ease though that comes with actually witnessing another Scottish side two up in a final on a foreign field. Words flowed. And even at half-time when often I had been summarising depressing results in the past I was now trying to restrain myself from even thinking that it really was all over at 2–0.

After Rangers went 3–0 up just nine minutes into the second-half, when a long clearance by goalkeeper Peter McCloy found an unchallenged Johnston again, who could not have missed finding the net, it did look like the Ibrox side were winning with an ease that really stumped me. That second goal changed the nature of the whole commentary which is why it sticks in the mind. 3–0 it was almost like you could lie back and think of words for the end that would convey a night of historic triumph. That was the chasm created. The Russians at that stage looked like stiff robots. No way back. I was actually looking ahead to a cup presentation and what I might say over the pictures of John Greig lifting the trophy. However, something else was happening. Three up, three crowd invasions. Rangers supporters would flood on, after each goal, wave their colours and then be ushered off again by the Guardia Civil, a body with a fearsome reputation in a fascist society but who were acting no more strongly than lollipop ladies ushering kids across a street. It was a paradox which only encouraged the view among the visitors that the pitch was simply there for the taking. Also, close to the action in my near-pitch position I could survey all of this clearly. In particular there was one small, portly man in a braided uniform which suggested higher rank of some note. But he never budged during the interruptions. Later he did with an effect that at the time reminded me of the mass start of the Grand National at Aintree.

Rangers' superiority was in such stark contrast to the other hard-fought victories in the previous games, that you really had to wonder now how the Russians had reached this level. As I was looking down at my fact-sheet and seeing names that were really unknown to me and beginning to look harmlessly more like the cast of a Chekhov play, two of them scored. Eshtrekov with half an hour to go, and Makhovikov with three minutes left. That last one causing a Rangers panic both on and off the field as if they had announced a wild dog was now on the loose in the stadium.

But the men with the Govan address stood firm and triumphed. Waves of supporters flooded on. The Guardia did make motions to usher them off but they were feckless until that little officer in front of my eyes gave a downward chop with his arm and thus sparked off that Aintree-like start as a long wave of Guardia Civil surged forward batons flailing to drive the Rangers fans back to the other side of the field. But, back the fans came, mistakenly and recklessly armed with wooden sticks taken from seats they had broken up on the spot. An ugly battle ensued where there was only ever going to be one winner. As it proceeded I talked to the Reuters' correspondent for the Catalan area who, after agreeing that drunken hooliganism was at the root of all this, added, 'What you are seeing down there is the fascist police in action. That is the only way they can handle such a disturbance. They are not even Catalan. They are from outside and brought into this area to maintain a dictatorship.'

As he was talking, the trophy was being presented to John Greig safely inside the stadium out of our sight by a UEFA official, who simply said to him, 'This is the European Cup Winners' Cup. Take it.' That almost indecent informality encapsulated the bizarre nature of that night in Barcelona where a football triumph had been reduced simply to an afterthought.

26

Studs to the Fore

Rangers v Celtic
3–2
Scottish Cup Final
5 May 1973
Goal: Tom Forsyth

IT'S A BIZARRE and almost comical goal that I trace back to anger and division. It was the day I heard a screaming argument going on above me as I was sitting downstairs in the marble lounge at Ibrox, waiting for an interview. I could hear the clash of voices above, that with indiscriminate language and thunderous conviction was, in fact, Willie Waddell, chief executive of Rangers engaged in a furious row with his manager Jock Wallace. There and then it seemed to have a consequence to it akin to the *Gunfight at the OK Corral*. That moment came to mind when shortly afterwards Wallace left Ibrox, bemusing a support who had witnessed him ending Celtic's nine-year dominance in the league, stopping them from reaching that mystical ten figure and ultimately winning two trebles thereafter. Enough to keep him there until retiral you would have thought. As it happened I was on the commentary platform on that May day when the whole rigmarole began for Wallace. And, I link it with the strangest goal I had ever witnessed at a cup final. A winning goal that you would not associate with spectacle or a trumpet voluntary to signify the start of a new triumphant era.

Indeed, in 1992 I invited both Jock Wallace and Jimmy Johnstone, near neighbours of mine in Lanarkshire, to my birthday party, hoping to be regaled by tales about that particular day when they were in opposition, as all of us would be in reminiscing mood. Jinky was his usual effervescent self. However, Jock was morose and hardly opened his mouth. It was eerie. He was a naturally ebullient man. When I asked Jinky about THE goal he laughed outright about it then went on singing like that was all he wanted to contribute.

For that day a winning goal was both a triumph for one side and an embarrassment for the other. Unsurprisingly Kenny Dalglish opened the scoring in 25 minutes for Celtic and the lead alternated, with Parlane and then Conn putting Rangers in the lead before the Connelly penalty in 52 minutes levelled the game at 2–2. Rangers looked better equipped for this under an uncompromising Wallace who could put the fear of death into a Bengal tiger, and believed a regular run up a steep sandhill could provide you with the elixir for long life.

The winner came from a man who was having a fine game at the other end of the field from the Celtic penalty area. This is what Alan Herron, of the *Sunday Mail* wrote of him that day, 'Tom Forsyth was a colossus. He tackled hard, he won the ball in the air and he won it on the ground.' Immensely popular on the Ibrox terracing he was hated by some of his opponents and Jock Stein was credited for saying of him that he should have been wearing a butcher's apron when he played.

So, how in the 60th minute did this player not only end up in the Celtic box, but actually on their goal-line? It was a free kick on the left taken immaculately by Tommy McLean which found the head of Derek Johnstone who sent the ball against the right-hand post from which it rolled slowly along the goal-line begging for company. I honestly cannot recall where the Celtic keeper was at that moment, or any Celtic defender, but Forsyth was almost on the goal-line with an initial reaction that seemed to hamper him. It was disbelief. A ball rolls along the line towards the unmarked feet of a Rangers defender on the Celtic goal-line? Life doesn't prepare you for quirks like that. So Forsyth's hesitant feet could not summon up a dramatic, thunderous *coup de grace*. Instead, his flurried touch to push it over the line was like he could not countenance hurting the feelings of his opponents who had graciously vanished to allow him to score his first ever Rangers goal and win the cup 3–2 in his first season.

I had tried to remind Jock Wallace of the goal and his triumph at the party that night. I thought it was modesty that constrained him from talking about it all. He did admit though that at the end of the game in the excitement he had walked past the outstretched hand of Bobby Murdoch which was seen clearly by television viewers. It led to him being criticised by his own mother for what appeared a deliberate snub. It was not until much later I was to discover that he was in the first stages of Parkinson's disease that unknown to us at my party that night, was the reason for him looking sadly like a lost soul.

27

Arthur's Warning

Scotland v Czechoslovakia
World Cup Qualifier
26 September 1973
2–1
Goal: Joe Jordan

ARTHUR MONTFORD OF Scottish Television and I were competitors in the broadcasting world but genuinely good friends who would play golf together occasionally where he always had the upper hand. There was one special evening when he used a phrase (a *cri de coeur*, in fact) that would make all my efforts commentating on the same game, seem quite tame. It was the evening of a World Cup qualifier when expectancy of qualifying was genuinely high but fraught with the traditional uncertainties that come with supporting Scotland. Their opponents were Czechoslovakia. Our manager was Willie Ormond had who been put in a favourable position by Tommy Docherty almost qualifying us for Germany, but who had departed for Old Trafford with the job still to be finished in a move which provoked contrasting views among the Scottish media, many of whom felt he had deserted the cause. The contrast between the two men could not have been greater. The Doc was greatly self-possessed, a bundle of energy with a quip to hand for any occasion and it never surprised me in later life that he became lauded as one of the UK's most accomplished after-dinner speakers. Ormond was a more self-contained man who spoke in quieter, measured tones but whose background as a member of the 'Famous Five' of Hibernian lent him a unique seal of approval over and above his splendid record as manager with St Johnstone whom he had taken to unprecedented levels.

Although, one of the most difficult games I ever had to cover was when, on an icily cold night in February just after his appointment, he was in charge of a Scotland side losing 5–0 to England at Hampden which sent shivers up the spine in more ways than one.

But now we had to beat the Czechs and that would be that. Which was why Arthur and I were on edge. The thought of going to our first World Cup finals made us feel a bit like debutantes hoping to be presented at court. The Czechs were no slouches. But they were apparently temperamental. They had dropped a point surprisingly in Copenhagen, a side we had put away with ease under the Doc. Thus the target was simple. Victory and we would be there.

Looking back I feel that the Scottish side wanted to prove their worth by doing it the hard way. For just after half an hour Zdeněk Nehoda who had been quiet up till then put in an angular shot from outside the penalty area which you would have imagined your grannie might have saved. Except, for some unaccountable reason Ally Hunter in goal fumbled the ball which went gracefully over the line. Stunned though I was I had to keep going and it was then Arthur created the words that caught the imagination of the public. Matters were getting serious and the rough and tumble was increasing, given the Czechs had been given a lifeline. Tackles were flying in and Billy Bremner, the Scottish captain and never one to avoid the midfield maelstrom, was getting rough treatment, which prompted Arthur to shout (as I was to hear later) in no uncertain manner, 'Watch your legs, Billy' as if he was now a punter on the terracing although, I am sure, reflecting the instinctive feelings of the viewing public.

The looped headed equaliser by big Jim Holton from a corner-kick just before half-time did not steady the nerves for we had to endure Bremner hitting the post before justice was served. It was just under 15 minutes to go when we were to rejoice at the sight of one of the most famous gap-toothed faces of all time beaming at us from the Hampden pitch. It belonged to Joe Jordan who bent low from a chip by Willie Morgan to head home the winner, then beamed his scarcity of teeth like he didn't give a damn about how he looked.

I would personally have paid for Jordan's dental treatment, and probably augmented with gold fillings, for getting me to Germany. And Billy did watch his legs to lead us to our first World Cup finals in 16 years.

28

Drawing a Line

Dundee v Celtic
1–0
Scottish League Cup Final
15 December 1973
Goal: Gordon Wallace

IT WAS THE day that started with a warning. 'Remember the 18-yard line,' my producer reminded me as we were driving to Hampden Park for this final in sleety rain which would not stop all day. A line was drawn across pitches 18 yards from the goal-line in a wide experiment intended to re-shape football. The off-side law would only apply within that area. It was the '70s' baleful attempt to make football less controversial and would lead only to the kind of recriminatory consequences that VAR was supposed to eliminate for good. Sir Stanley Rous, the President of FIFA was present to witness how effective it would be. It was to be of no significance. But I suspect Rous himself was. And the damnable weather and the British state being in paralysis, certainly were.

The sudden rise in the oil price, and the subsequent shortage that produced an economic crisis had led to emergency conservation regulations that had forced this match to kick off at 1.30 instead of 3pm to avoid the use of the floodlights. And when we arrived at Hampden the pitch was a blend of ice and water. Bobby Davidson from Airdrie was the referee who had inspected the pitch and I was surprised it had been judged playable. Now Davidson and Jock Stein the Celtic manager were as matey as Punch and Judy and I expected enough heat to generate between them about that decision as would create the impression of an imminent thaw. I suspect though that the presence of the plenipotentiary from FIFA and the useless experiment may have prevented the ref from telling Rous, 'Gemme's aff!'

Early in the match I had to make mention of the paltry crowd of 27,974 that had turned up looking like volunteers in an Arctic clothing experiment, huddling mostly on the north terracing and minus many from Dundee who under fuel-emergency conditions, and foul weather, simply could not travel. It was a thought as Celtic, minus the surprisingly benched Jimmy Johnstone and George Connelly, took to the field.

Half chances that never seemed like preludes to goals matched the dreariness of sub-Arctic Hampden. And perhaps the long ball was being over-used by Celtic, as I recall, to take advantage of this off-side experiment. Or not, as the case may be, for as the game progressed I felt Dundee were like a team growing in self-awareness and beginning to realise they hadn't turned up merely for the chop. Danny McGrain I recall clearing a Gordon Wallace shot off the line and I certainly could not miss Kenny Dalglish shooting straight into the arms of the Dundee keeper Thomson Allan which normally would have had him turning away in triumph arms aloft. So this was a day when the customary images were absent. Rather like watching a serial on television and your favourite characters are absent from a single episode.

Two images did shine through the dreariness of a Hampden which seemed increasingly like nature was in a conspiracy to turn it into a torture chamber with the thought of all of this going to extra-time in the unceasing rain and the seeping cold. The first came 14 minutes from the end. It was one of those goals that comes along in a tight no-scoring game to make you realise, despite all the preceding negative efforts, scoring goals can be absurdly simple. Gordon Wallace managed to chest down a free kick in defiance of the Celtic defence. He had his back to goal. His turn and low shot eluded Ally Hunter in goal. Simply executed. Dundee were in front and stayed there. 1–0 to lift the cup against all expectations. The second image was the cup presentation when the man who scored the goal in Lisbon for Celtic lifted the cup, as manager of Dundee, in front of mostly men who had followed him through thick and thin in a green and white jersey. Viewing his demeanour, I suspected Tommy Gemmell had not discarded his past lightly. For I recall him afterwards in an interview nursing professional contentment but certainly not wallowing in public triumph that is the normal corollary of a cup win. Sunny Lisbon in refrigerated Hampden was difficult to forget. The Wallace goal though meant he could detach himself from the past with a broad, guiltless smile on his face.

29

Sassenach Intervention

Scotland v England
2–0
Home International
18 May 1974
Goal: Colin Todd (OG)

It was the sweetest of OGs. Or so I thought at the time. One of those had to be included, in my compendium of goals, that clung on for weeks after. Especially Auld Enemy OGs. They were greeted by the vast majority of 93,271 inside Hampden that day, like ecstatic kids at Christmas receiving totally unexpected gifts from a distant relative. In fact there were two OGs that day but the second one bothered me particularly in a strange way. The game had significance well beyond the domestic UK parameters. Scotland were heading for Germany and the World Cup finals. England were not. And in case they had forgotten that fact, throughout the 90 minutes the Hampden crowd constantly reminded them of it, in tuneful ditties of which Cole Porter would have been proud. And, despite the almost comical pre-match publicity which the Scottish squad had received, this was a devoted, faithful support as represented by a punter who addressed me on the way to the commentary position with words that were not intended to inspire me. 'You lot are scum! You are all trying to destroy the wee man, and just before a World Cup too.'

He was referring clearly to the Scotland winger Jimmy Johnstone. And yes, the Scottish press had not portrayed him as a conscientious worker, slaving away to hone his skills for the big test. Instead, the Scottish papers were splashed, front-page and back, about how Jinky had taken a rowing boat out from the seafront at Largs, during preparation for the England game, lost his oars and had to be picked up by the air and sea rescue people. But there were particular press-men there who could make a story out of someone spilling soup over a tablecloth. So this was too good to miss. Yes, it didn't look good. But those of us who knew Jinky well realised that such publicity might hurt him deeply.

Certainly, it did not affect his manager. At that stage, before the experiences in Germany, he was devoted to the wee man. So out Jimmy trotted onto Hampden that afternoon to an acclamation that was like he was to be Scotland's rowing representative at the next Olympics. And within minutes he was bamboozling an England defence which, for the first and perhaps only time I can recollect, looked almost deferential to this Scotland side who were leaving them behind on these shores in a few weeks' time. And that was also because England went behind so early in the match. In only five minutes Joe Jordan, now a national hero for stamping our passport for Germany, gathered a rebound inside the penalty area and with the keeper off his line let fly. I think it might have gone astray but for the intervention of defender Mike Pejic who stretched out a leg to divert it away from his keeper who was left to lift the ball sheepishly out of the back of the net.

Now you might have thought that everything else was academic. After all we were preparing for a World Cup in a few weeks' time, this result need not have mattered. But this was the Auld Enemy. They were only ever against us to be beaten and they still had talented players. So the outcome still hung in the balance. Then just on the half-hour with Scotland increasing pressure Peter Lorimer swept a low ball across the penalty area which I am sure would have found the keeper, except that Colin Todd replicated Pejic by stretching out a leg, like an instinctive striker, and the ball landed up in the English net. 2–0. That final result led to a demonstration which I did not think augured well for relationships in Germany. For forming in the centre-circle after the final whistle the Scottish players gave unmistakable two-finger salutes to the Hampden press-box. But Todd's goal, thereafter, haunted me in a strange way. We had enjoyed a considerable share of luck in that match underlined by his intervention. Had fate dealt its last hand to us? Would we be without good luck in a tournament where I suspected it might be badly needed? I wasn't to be far wrong in my misgivings out of a single OG.

30

The First Hiccup

Belgium v Scotland
2–1
Pre-World Cup warm-up game
1 June 1974
Goal: Jimmy Johnstone

LET ME ADMIT that my first thought on accompanying the Scottish players on the plane to Brussels in June 1974 and watching them disembark at the airport was that they were as high as kites. Certainly the nation as a whole was experiencing a World Cup euphoria in which there seemed to be less antagonism in the air and the lollipop lady who normally scowled at me as I drove past the local school actually smiled on one occasion. The local butcher, for instance, thanked me for my post-match comments on the qualification by giving me a roast, gratis, like I had rubbished vegetarianism on the air. And, I suppose, the players' celebrations were fully understandable. But now only a couple of weeks away from their first game in Dortmund against Zaire on 19 June most of them looked hungover in their first steps on the continent.

British Airways had not helped by lavishing drink on all of us on the flight to Brussels. For nobody in the media had signed the pledge either. Myself? I walked down the gangway with a bottle of champagne in each hand. And I put it to good use.

It was not until I saw Billy Bremner leading out his side in the small stadium in Bruges a couple of days later that I felt there had been a lot more drinking going on than just on the flight. And, of course, because of the Johnstone incident most of the media were now regarded as aliens. So

I didn't meet anybody who enjoyed that game. It was actually beginning to feel like THEM and US. Although privately Jinky, because of my personal relations with him, did talk to me. I spoke to him in Glasgow Airport before departure and his use of 'bastard' about certain press-men was prolific.

I didn't think it was healthy but there was no way I was going to shy away from any chat with any of the players. So I was interested to see how Jinky would fare in this outing, and how mentally he had really been affected. Well, Scotland's performance creaked and the Belgians were typically organised, but without any real flair. Not that the game was going to need that for we made the charitable assumption that Scotland would be playing well within themselves. The fact that they went a goal down in 22 minutes from a goal by a Roger Henrotay did not phase anybody. And then, as if it had been scripted by an associate of Jinky, the wee winger scored the equaliser with a shot the goalkeeper could only blink at as it passed him. That was just before half-time and yet again there was a clenched fist directed towards the press-box. The fact that Belgium were to go on and win 2–1 through a penalty ten minutes from the end was much less significant than this fractured relationship between players and the media. It began to look as if only a bridge builder like Thomas Telford could span the gap between us. And I especially wondered how Jinky in particular might be affected by all of this in the pressurised climate of the World Cup itself.

Surely, that precious goal was a manifestation of a man in the right frame of mind and ready to deliver and that the manager would have seen him now as an irreplaceable asset. So most of us thought at the time. Having known the wee man personally since he lived around my parts and had occasional drinks with him and mutual friends I simply believed he would meet the challenge. His manager Willie Ormond had other ideas.

31

The Odd Couple

Norway v Scotland
1–2
Pre-World Cup Friendly
6 June 1974
Goal: Kenny Dalglish

THIS MATCH RESONATES for me in a strange way. When I think of it I cannot avoid the images of chaos that preceded it off the park amongst the Scotland squad and the fact that the scorer of the chosen goal was like a Trappist monk compared to others. After the anti-climax of the Belgium game it should have been a 'sobering' experience for us, except, looking back, that would have been an injudicious use of the English language given what was to ensue in the land of the fiords. Scotland were housed in a student hostel attached to the university alive with tall willowy blondes who seemed to be studying Dior rather than Descartes and gave rise to how our young lads might respond. But as far as we know it could have been a nunnery for all that occurred. Straying was of a different variety. One evening having a drink in a student tavern with the English commentator John Motson, we were joined by the Scotland captain Billy Bremner and Jimmy Johnstone, 'roarin' fu'. They could hardly stand. The Scotland doctor intervened to drag them out of the place although the word got out and the squad had to face up to an international match with a public storm breaking over their heads about the misconduct of their captain and a star player. Did they really have any sense of responsibility?

Now Norway, as such, did not represent the greatest of challenges and were seen simply as a stepping stone on the inevitable route to Germany.

They had one outstanding player, their striker Tom Lund whom many regard as their finest ever player and was pursued by every major club in Europe including Bayern and Real Madrid. We knew hardly anything of the others but immediately in the game could see that they were no slouches. Despite the warnings that had been given it was indeed Lund who opened the scoring when he chased after a long ball from his keeper and nipped it past Tom Allan in goal in 19 minutes. Thus, we waited for a response which seemed as if it would never materialise and started to think about how to excuse another defeat, like in Belgium. I was preparing the viewers by suggesting that when the time would come we would really be up for it and you would see a 'different' Scotland although with no great belief myself. But sometimes you have to fill a vacuum as creatively as you can.

And then, the captain, who could hardly stand upright a couple of nights before, stepped into the breach, suggesting his internal organs seemed to thrive on the hard stuff. With 15 minutes remaining his free kick found the head of Joe Jordan who breached their defence. 1–1. The winning goal came from contrasting personalities. Bremner again took a free kick which was headed on by Jordan, for Kenny Dalglish to nip in and squeeze it past the keeper. Compared to other Kenny goals in his career it would be of lowly ranking. But nothing could have been more appropriate for him to have scored our last pre-World Cup goal for 2–1. For he had been a model of astute professionalism throughout the preparations. But, at least publicly, not a word escaped his lips about his captain or about the capricious and unpredictable nature of his club colleague. He went about looking solemn at times compared to others, his mind focused clearly on his pursuit of perfection on the field. Despite his winning goal though we were entering a World Cup with soured relations between many of the players and the media. So we were decidedly uneasy now about our prospects. That goal by Jordan at Hampden against the Czechs, to qualify us for the finals, seemed to be entirely unrelated to this squad. They seemed a different lot.

When I met my co-commentator for the first time in Germany, Jock Stein, I recall his first words, 'What the f--- has been going on?' He didn't like what I had to say except about how his player Kenny Dalglish had been a stand-out.

32

Raising the Temperature

Scotland v Zaire
2–0
World Cup
14 June 1974
Goal: Peter Lorimer

On the eve of Scotland's opening game against Zaire I sensed there was, if not a wholehearted effort to let bygones be bygones, at least a slight lessening of the tension between 'THEM and US', from what we could determine at the earlier press conferences in Germany. Our opening game was against Zaire, or the 'wee darkies' as the Scotland manager Willie Ormond would describe them. This lessening might have stemmed from the meeting I had with Jock Stein and Billy Bremner in a Dortmund café two days before Zaire. The Celtic manager listened to all of Bremner's complaints about Ormond for a few minutes then put a large fist below Bremner's chin and gave him a verbal fusillade that had me shaking on the other side of the table. The message was simple. Stop your moaning. Play for the country not for the media. Don't let yourselves down. It was a strength of character that I don't think Ormond had in him. And it was definitely sobering. The one question Stein asked the captain with intent was, 'How's Denis?'

He was referring to Scotland's record goalscorer who was then at the grand old age of 34 and treated with reverence by all and sundry in the camp and highly popular with the media, some of whom he had known since he started out in the business with Scotland in 1958. This would be his 55th cap if he were selected and although he had been given a thumbs up by Bremner, and Stein pursued it no further, the Celtic manager had serious reservations about the veteran's suitability. But he was selected and given the heat and humidity on the night of the game you would have been perplexed about anybody's suitability. On the platform we sweated profusely under the canopy of the stand and wondered if this would all be to the benefit of the Africans.

But apart from one or two flourishes they were a class well below our players. This Law was clearly not the Denis Law of popular adoration. Far from it. Was it his advanced age or simply the conditions? I didn't mention him much in commentary and it was frustrating to see a renowned almost legendary figure suffering from self-inflicted anonymity. As Scotland continued to dominate they announced their presence through the figure of Peter Lorimer who presented us with something we had waited all of 16 years for, a World Cup goal. The last one had been scored by the diminutive figure of Celtic's Bobby Collins against Paraguay. In the 27th minute the ball stood up nicely for Peter Lorimer, the Leeds player with a renowned power of shot, and demonstrated it here in spectacular fashion by driving the ball into the roof of the net from just inside the penalty area.

I think I felt a sense of relief coming off Jock Stein beside me, that they had overcome growing frustration. And when Joe Jordan scored only eight minutes later it seemed like we were cruising. In a sense we were and could have added perhaps one more but instead the principal feature was Scotland either incapable of mounting pressure, or deliberately conserving energy. It was not until later in the tournament that we looked back on the opening match and criticism surfaced about why they didn't press home the clear supremacy we had over the 'wee darkies'. Why be satisfied with only 2–0? Lorimer's stunning goal tended to be forgotten in such arguments. But, there is little doubt that it inspired a new confidence in the squad which you could clearly detect. Although I suspected there would be one issue settled. For coming down from our commentary position Stein said simply of Denis, 'He's finished.' It was his last game for his country and he spectated with a grudge, the next game against Brazil which ended goalless in the Waldstadion with the memory stained by finding it difficult to forget Billy Bremner's complete miss of the ball only a few feet in front of the Brazil goal which at the time you felt a primary school kid could have converted. If that stung it was nothing like the experience of our exit from the World Cup in a way which forced you to suspend rationality and conclude that somebody up there definitely doesn't like us.

33

A New Kind of Pain

Scotland v Yugoslavia
1–1
22 June 1974
Goal: Joe Jordan

ONE OF SCOTLAND'S most experienced and hardened journalists Hugh Taylor of the *Scottish Daily Record* admitted to me after our final World Cup game that the ending brought tears to his eyes. Scotland were in the Waldstadion again facing Yugoslavia this time as Brazil were playing the 'wee darkies' Zaire at another venue. It was the last seven minutes of this game that crushed many Scottish spirits. That the Slavs had demolished Zaire 9–0 in their match previously was mainly down to the strange attitude of the Zaire coach who in a dispute about cash, with his association, selected a goalkeeper who was the size of Jimmy Johnstone which their opponents could scarcely fail to notice. The goals duly followed. We were newcomers to the World Cup but we knew that to make absolutely certain of qualification we would have to win this game whilst Yugoslavia could settle for a draw. On this occasion I was minus Jock Stein as co-commentator. He had been taken away to work for BBC London, given the assumption by them that Scotland's chances of qualification were zero. On the night before he left for his other duty I recall having a long conversation about Kenny Dalglish. He was obviously an admirer of Kenny but had been disappointed in his performances so far and even wondered if he would be selected for the last game, but he eventually was in an unchanged Scotland side. In these circumstances I had given up hope of a Scottish qualification. Then as the game proceeded news began to filter back from the Brazil–Zaire game where there was no avalanche of goals as we had expected. In our game the Yugoslavs were extremely physical. Given Billy Bremner's reputation as Scotland's director of operations and hard man, I recall them going after him in a big way. They had obviously watched his miss against Brazil in the previous match and wanted him neutralised. They succeeded, as Scotland increasingly found it difficult to pierce a fierce Yugoslav defence. A chance did fall to Jordan in the first half when Sandy Jardine having perhaps his best game in a Scotland jersey had a shot blocked by defender Katalinski, with the rebound falling to the Scotland striker only yards from goal. He seemed to stab at it, but the keeper, well out of his goal parried it at his feet. Then came the sickener with only seven minutes of the game remaining. Danny McGrain, with almost painstaking professionalism admits he was at fault.

'I thought my opponent didn't have much of a left foot. So when he received his pass I forced him to turn to that. But didn't he send over a great cross with that particular foot which beat Sandy Jardine and the Yugoslav there headed it into the net. I felt sore about that because it had put them in the lead.'

It was Karasi's head which did the damage and they were now 1–0 up with only nine minutes remaining and I felt like I had been consumed by an emotional landslide. But an even more aggravating moment was to follow. With one minute remaining Tommy Hutchison who had come on for the under-performing Dalglish sent a ball into a crowded Yugoslav penalty area which just eluded Lorimer but broke to Jordan who scooped it up into the air in front of him and then poked the ball between the keeper and the post for the equaliser. What struck me at the same time was that the last I had heard Brazil were only leading Zaire by 2–0. And if that were the case then Joe Jordan had just qualified us for the next round. An elation that so far had eluded me swept through me like I had inherited wealth unexpectedly from a distant relative. But was it still 2–0 in the other game as I believed at that moment. The Jordan goal loomed like a monument to salvation in the mind. It was not until the Scottish players were in the dressing room that they had heard that Brazil had scored a third and they were thus out of the competition having only scored two against Zaire. Perhaps some tears emerging even from experienced journalists was put into perspective eventually when all was done and dusted we learned that we were the first country to be eliminated from a World Cup finals without having lost a match.

Of course, the lack of goals in the opening Zaire match took up much of the inquest that followed which simply underlined how naïve our approach had been to our first World Cup commitment. There was inevitably a degree of journalistic criticism but what we could not have foreseen was the public reaction. I recall returning on the aircraft to Glasgow Airport with the squad when the captain announced on our descent that there was a crowd awaiting us. We could scarcely believe it with sense the sense of failure in the cabin being as thick as a soup. But thousands had turned out to our amazement. They greeted us like we had returned with honour. I have never seen a group of players reviving from glum indifference to almost joyful gratitude in such a short space of time as they walked through the throngs eventually with perhaps an underpinning of collective embarrassment. Recalling Joe's goal in those circumstances simply fed into our belief that we had been hard done by and that we were fit company for any World Cup.

34

Breaking the Mould

England v Scotland
1–2
Home International
4 June 1977
Goal: Gordon McQueen

FOOTBALL PRESS CONFERENCES are usually cliché hidebound. They never were at Ally MacLeod's. Nobody yawned in his. I was at a special one only a few weeks after he had been appointed Scotland manager in May 1977 (an appointment about which at the time Jock Stein said to me, 'It's a joke'). It was a few days before he led his Scotland side to Wembley against the Auld Enemy. He didn't hold back. To a question about how he felt managing against England for the first time he replied, 'I don't dislike the English. I hate their guts'. The English couldn't see the funny side of that remark, and neither did some of his kith and kin. For he repeated it for me in front of camera. But that was Ally for you who didn't seem to care that he was tempting providence by such a remark.

The English were preparing for the Scots both on and off the field. The MP for Brent North, inside of which Wembley was sited, told the London *Evening Standard*, 'Lock up your doors and batten down your windows for the Wembley-bound Scots are dangerous.' Inflammatory? By some degree. Nevertheless I had witnessed myself, at past Wembleys some violent conduct by supporters who were disgracing the tartan. I actually saw cars being overturned in Soho on the eve of one game by men garbed in our colours and clearly pissed out of their minds.

So, into a potential maelstrom, as some English saw it, stepped one of the most flamboyant figures in British football, Ally MacLeod, who had touched the side of his prominent nose on the day of his appointment and said to the press, 'Concorde has landed.' His public loved it. What his players thought of it all would depend on his results and particularly his baptism at Wembley.

On a brilliantly sunny day you could tell early on that the Scottish players were reflecting the spirit of their manager by taking the game to the English and with Dalglish in particular looking sprightly and playing his last game as a Celtic player before leaving for Liverpool, the omens were good. Then came the goal after which I thought we would not lose this game. I doubt if I had ever been as confident in Wembley before with so long to go, since the Scottish goal was scored two minutes from half-time.

It came from the head of the jovial giant Gordon McQueen when, from a tempting ball in the air across the English goal, he rose majestically to power a header past the keeper. It was one of those headers that make you feel the opponents have been kicked in the teeth. My confidence, surprisingly, soared. Then when Dalglish nipped in to score a scrappy kind of goal for 2–0 on the hour mark, I felt that was it. Not even a Mick Channon penalty three minutes from time to make it 2–1 dented me. It was too late for them.

Then came the 'celebrations'. I still cling on to that word despite what was to happen. The first trickle of a pitch invasion by our supporters turned into a veritable flood until you could hardly see a blade of grass under their feet. Then I noticed the posts being climbed and fans sitting along the crossbar. Bouncing on it seemed like innocent fun. I then realised another interpretation was developing behind me. I heard Jonathan Martin, the BBC's Head of Sport, bawling instructions to 'get the focus on the mob on the crossbar'. When I saw it sag for the last time and then snap I realised my English colleagues were actually relishing this, as if they were grasping the opportunity to expose what Scots were really like. For being defeated by a side supported by ruffians like that was simply unacceptable.

But that was my tribe down there. I wasn't enjoying watching these supporters destroying the crossbars and digging up the pitch in places. But neither did I approve of the way some of my BBC colleagues were enjoying launching attacks on the support. So I admit I let the pictures tell their own story without too much colouring by me.

It was in Argentina the following year in the World Cup in that horrible hotel the Scots team were resident in, that I spoke to the amiable Gordon McQueen about how his goal had affected me and others and how the breaking of the crossbar with the criticism that followed affected him. He poured out a torrent of praise for the Scottish support. Here he was on the other side of the Atlantic with events not going to plan and he was missing the proximity and robustness of the Scottish support. 'We could well do with them here,' he said. 'They know better than anybody when and how to party. This World Cup doesn't know what it's missing.' Uttered at one of the lowest points in the tournament and sounding to me like an invalid being denied his oxygen supply.

35

The Finest Touch

Wales v Scotland
0–2
World Cup Qualifier
12 October 1977
Goal: Kenny Dalglish

WE REALISED THE vast Scottish support crammed inside Anfield, Liverpool that evening were in specially vociferous voice when they were able to drown out the blarings of the pre-match Welsh Guards band. But there was another factor intriguing my co-commentator who, sweeping his gaze around a crowd crushed onto the terracing in such numbers you had to wonder if they were all in there legally, muttered to me, 'I hope to God we win. If we don't I think they'll take Liverpool apart!' He was Jock Stein who was not entirely ignorant of the ways of the unrestrained emotions of supporters and sensed an element of desperation in these voices. We both were also aware that some travelling Scottish supporters for Wembley games in the past had acted in parts of London like Viking raiders, so that awful prospect added to the tension of the evening.

Of course, before the game we had a pre-match discussion with some Welsh journalists who pointed out to us the simple reason we were playing a decider on English soil. 'It should have been at Wrexham,' one of them declared to me but pointing to the gathering masses, added, 'It was about money.' Either in the Welsh language or plain English the meaning was clear, it was a sell-out. In more ways than one.

The Scottish thousands were clearly the 'home' crowd. With that kind of support Scotland dominated the game but as time passed and we missed an array of solid chances the feeling grew that we were sliding slowly towards anti-climax, even though it was clearly evident we were the superior side. And, indeed, Alan Rough had to make one of the saves of his life when he tipped a John Toshack volley over the bar late on in the game, in one of the Welshmen's rare attacks. With 11 minutes left came the incident that caused me some sleepless nights for many weeks after, as I wrestled with thoughts which were guilt ridden. It was what caused a Don Masson penalty. The nocturnal mayhem was caused by my recalling vividly what I had said in commentary with only about 12 minutes left. Two players had risen to a ball floated into the penalty area, the Welsh centre-half Dave Jones and our striker Joe Jordan. Hands went up. Penalty. The referee decided that instantly. The Welsh protested, especially Jones. In commentary I endorsed the referee's decision almost with acclaim. After all I was speaking to the largest audience for a football match in the history of BBC Scotland broadcasting – later worked out at 95 per cent of the viewing public, so, admittedly I might have been influenced by the circumstances, as there is dubiety about that decision has endured through the decade, and listening back to that event I wish I had been less adamant.

Now I have met Joe many times since, but only once or twice has the subject arisen and when it did he assured me he didn't handle and I take some comfort in that. But only some. If VAR had been involved we might have been there until midnight.

And the penalty taken by Masson was classically cool and wrongfooted Dai Davies in goal. 'Thank God,' a voice beside me uttered off-mike. Stein and I were now feeling as if we had just emerged from a torture chamber. It meant so much. Then to lift us in the manner that was befitting of the occasion came Kenny. Three minutes remaining Martin Buchan ventures down the right and his cross is with power. The manner in which Dalglish met it with his head was like it could not have been stopped by a wire-mesh strung from post to post. A goal that sent us to Argentina 2–0 and sent me into a paroxysm of commentating delight which deserved the Pavarotti award for hitting one of the highest notes in broadcasting history.

36

A Political Stew

Chile v Scotland
2–4
Friendly international prior to World Cup in Argentina
15 June 1977
Goal: Lou Macari

THE PRIEST FROM the missionary in the outskirts of Santiago in Chile pointed out to me, in tones he might have adopted for consoling a grieving parent, the bullet holes in the wall made by the state's secret police who had been trying to capture Dr Sheila Cassidy. She had been in that country both providing medical help to the poor and engaging in missionary work. Her revelations to the rest of the world of the brutalities of the fascist police ended up with her being tortured almost to the point of death in 1975, two years before an SFA entourage landed with a Scotland team to play in the National Stadium. Along with other journalists and broadcasters I was part of that group who were being mercilessly criticised, along with the football dignitaries, for apparently helping legitimise a ruthless dictatorship by simply stepping foot in that country. It was also widely known that the National Stadium in the city where the friendly international game was to be played had been used as a concentration camp during the fascist uprising and that blood had literally been spilled on its surface.

So, those of us who had decided to travel were faced by a high volume of moral outrage that stretched from angry parliamentarians to the local ministry, one of whom accosted me in a coffee bar in my home village with a message that seemed to be instructing me again in the meaning of the 30 pieces of silver betrayal. I hid behind my excuse that as this was part of a South American tour with the host nation Argentina and Brazil to be our opponents as well as that I was contracted to commit to this. In fact, I wanted to go, despite the outrage. We could, after all, report honestly on what we would experience and witness. Which was underlined by the Australian missionary saying to me at the bullet-riddled wall, 'Well, you're seeing it with your own eyes.'

Even our footballers were staggered by what they saw and Kenny Dalglish treated a smooth-talking apologist for the dictatorship, and who had come to our hotel to try to promote the idea that the views on his country were being distorted. Kenny treated that man with the disdain he normally reserved for English defenders and I recall him saying to this phoney, 'Bugger off, we'll make up our own minds'.

Indeed, the night of the game itself actually brought an instant recollection of the Ibrox disaster in January 1971 when 66 people died on stairway 13. There was a chilly, damp mist hanging around the National Stadium, as it had that afternoon in Govan, which seemed to thin the blood, or perhaps, in another sense, intensify the feeling of guilt about watching a game of football in a stadium where people had been tortured. But, with the mike in hand, it was just another game for me. We tried hard to concentrate on football. I had one sentence prepared in advance that I hoped and trusted I could use. On an evening when Scotland won with reasonable ease 4–2 and were three up at half-time, thankfully my prepared words came early in the game. I spouted, 'And there it is. A historic goal. The first Scotland goal ever on South American soil.' This on the continent where we had imported our 'passing' game. Well, you do have to clutch at straws at times.

It had come from the foot of Lou Macari to a deathly silence in this almost ghostly stadium where it was announced to the world that 60,000 were in the stadium. One-tenth of that would have been an exaggeration, thus indicating the Chilean FA were complicit with the regime in attempting to use even a football attendance to falsify reality.

Lou himself told me afterwards that the players had seen the bullet holes sprayed along some of the walls in the stadium but when I told him that he had made history he perked up a little because he was intensely a competitor above all else. It was also Scotland's 16th game with only one defeat in that time. It buoyed the manager Ally MacLeod to take on the World Cup finals' host Argentina next, in another country which paid little heed to a ballot-box.

37

Delusion

Argentina v Scotland
1–1
Pre-World Cup Friendly
18 June 1977
Goal: Don Masson

IN THE HOURS after the game in the steeply-sided, cavernous Boca Juniors stadium, Buenos Aires, filled with 57,000 ranting Argentines, I kept thinking of the evolutionists and the core of their thinking based on the concept of 'the survival of the fittest' – survival being the key word in any description of what unfolded on that pitch. The statistics which show that Argentina committed 41 fouls against us, to our 14, tells us little of the nature of the wildness of tackling that seemed to suggest that they felt the Scots were still cave dwellers. I mean when you consider the names of the players who were on the pitch wearing the strident Argentinian colours, Passarella, Ardiles, Houseman, Larrosa and particularly the striker Luque, whom Jock Stein would rave about to me, it's difficult to reason out why they were so viciously cynical that night. For these same men would play in the finals with grace, style and panache that made them invincible by simply sticking to the best precepts of our game.

It may have been that their dour, chain-smoking manager César Menotti held some ancient grudge against the Scots and his team-talk carried a license to maim. The most obvious thug was Vicente Pernía, the full-back, who spat in Willie Johnston's face and dug an elbow into the winger's kidney, slyly – he thought – but, in Johnston's angry reaction both players were sent off by the Brazilian referee in the 56th minute. We looked on worrying that a serious injury might befall one of ours, but at the same time realising gradually that Scotland were more than holding their own, and down below me I could see a greatly agitated Ally MacLeod semaphoring his dislike of proceedings to Menotti, still puffing away like he was calmly watching a tango display. But, underneath his concern, Ally was drinking in the fact that his side were in no way inferior to the host nation. He was storing that thought away for further use. And, of course, he danced with delight when Kenny Dalglish was brought down in the box by a defender, blatantly. A penalty, with only 13 minutes to go. And although this reward did not carry the weight and significance of what had occurred at Anfield, nevertheless, here was an opportunity to go in front of the host World Cup nation of formidable reputation.

Masson again seemed impervious to such significance and coolly put Scotland in front. Now Tom Forsyth in defence had been outstanding for Scotland in recent games. However, there were journalists in our camp who were sympathetic to a much publicised comment made about the defender back home, that he ought to wear a butcher's apron when he played. For only three minutes after the Scotland goal, when Forsyth tackled Oscar Trossero in the box, his reputation might have preceded him, for the referee pointed to the penalty spot. Even the cynics about Forsyth could hardly believe that decision. It was a Brazilian referee of course and the South American ethos might have been in play. Passarella placed it away. 1–1. There was no more scoring.

When Menotti came down to the press conference and refused to answer any questions about the crudities we had witnessed from his side the Scottish press walked out in protest which forced Alfredo Cantilo, the Argentine FA president to apologise and said he was ashamed of the performance. When it came Ally's turn I am witness to the fact that it was there and then he first released the vapours of fantasy which in truth we all inhaled, culminating in an epidemic which encouraged thousands to turn up at Hampden before the finals the following year just to wave the squad farewell. For that day he talked about his players as potential World Cup winners. That draw, that Masson penalty, had set this most amiable of men on the rockiest road anyone could follow; self-deception. He was not to travel alone in that delusionary manner.

38

Hanging by a Thread

Rangers v Aberdeen
2–1
Scottish Cup Final
6 May 1978
Goal: Steve Ritchie

IT WAS THE Aberdeen goal in the dying embers of this final which would bring to mind eventually the plight of a Rangers manager. A goal that did nothing to alter the outcome, but reminded me of what was happening at Ibrox. Long before that moment I stood with Billy McNeill, the Aberdeen manager, in the tunnel-mouth of Hampden Stadium about half an hour or so before this final. His eyes were sweeping round the terracings and eventually they focused on the massive Rangers support who were occupying two-thirds of the space. 'Look at that,' he said, 'That's their big advantage. When you have got that sort of crowd your players get a right lift'.

I realised there and then that his praise for his great, traditional rivals was simply linked to how much he was missing being backed that day by the massive hordes in green and white who had lent parity of support to him in the past on other cup final days. However much respect he had for the Aberdeen folk backing him that day he was admitting that an inspiring, uplifting factor that he had taken for granted in his previous career was crucially missing. Although, it has to be stated he loved working for the people in the club and he and his wife had assimilated into the Aberdeen way of life with great satisfaction. So I thought, at the time, it was nothing more than a surfacing of a piece of nostalgia that would evaporate at kick-off. Astonishingly, he revealed it was more than a passing thought. 'In my dressing room I've got Bobby Clark, one of my most experienced players and yet I can tell he's a bundle of nerves. I've got to do in there what Jock Wallace doesn't need to, and that's to try and lift them.' He spoke with clearly painful regret. I had almost to pinch myself, given that Billy had been voted Manager of the Year that season.

When I eventually climbed up to my commentary position I made no mention of what I considered an off-the-record conversation but I admit it did affect me. I had heard the almost stock phrase before, 'They lost the game before a ball was kicked,' as a way of dismissing a team's apparent puny efforts. An irresistible thought came into my mind as I placed commentary notes on top of a camera-case and looked down on the 61,563 crowd. It never left me throughout the entire game. And it was simply that I knew something about this final that the customers didn't down there. There was no way I could see Aberdeen winning given their manager was actually pining for the good old days that he felt his current team could not measure up to.

Most of my colleagues in the media were predicting a win for Rangers anyway, as they were only a game away from gaining the treble that season. On top of that they were managed by Jock Wallace who since he had taken over from Willie Waddell in 1972 had gained enormous respect from friend and foe alike, for his openness, his straight-backed resolution and success. It had apparently given him an impregnable position in Govan. The winning of this cup would be icing on the celebratory cake. So it seemed. All in all I sat there expecting a formality that day, given the mood in the Aberdeen dressing room and that the Dons would be facing a Rangers team where every player was an internationalist except one. And that was Bobby Russell who had been signed from my old favourites Shettleston Juniors and wasn't far short of international level and displayed it with a subtlety in his play that afternoon that even caused me to rate him above that of John Greig, playing his last ever game in a blue jersey.

I don't know whether I was also influenced by eagerly anticipating following Scotland to the World Cup finals in Argentina, later that month, but my overall impression was of a lukewarm final devoid of that customary pressure that can play havoc with my bladder which is so susceptible to drama and tension, especially in a Hampden press-box where queuing for the boy's room was inevitable. So when Alex MacDonald scored with a flying header in the 35th minute from an immaculate Russell chip into the box, I thought the deluge would follow. It didn't, but in a sense it was all over because I saw nothing of a responsive fight by the Dons. And when Derek Johnstone with a typical thunderous header scored the second with just over half an hour left we could have wrapped up and gone home. Except the game had an ending that was to intrigue me, not at the time, but weeks later when Ibrox was hit by a domestic upset, that was like an episode from *Succession*.

With only five minutes remaining a goal was scored by Aberdeen that clung to me as a portrayal of what had been occurring within Ibrox. A ball scooped up in the air by Steve Ritchie of the Dons rose and then floated like an escaped balloon as if to glance the crossbar. The tall Rangers goalkeeper Peter McCloy leapt, and as if to escort it to safety clutched at the bar and swung there dangling, pendulum-like for what seemed like an eternity before we all realised with him that he had only paved the way for the ball to drop down over the line. 2–1. So the game had ended in a kind of chuckle that made no difference to the outcome. John Greig had just won his sixth Winners' Cup final medal in his last game and Wallace had his second treble, the only Rangers manager to have done so. But then that swinging on the crossbar took on a new meaning for me and perhaps others close to the Ibrox scene.

For remarkably two weeks later Wallace left Ibrox with almost indecent haste from a job for which he was now being idolised but crucially wrenching himself free from the clutches of his mentor Willie Waddell. Wallace had been left dangling for months trying to grip on to his job under pressure from the Rangers chief executive who was a radically changed man. The combination of the Ibrox disaster when he had commendably held the club together and nursed it back to stability and the Barcelona riot which had entailed arduous but fruitful negotiations with many including UEFA to minimise consequences had taken its toll. Pressure had remoulded him, as others like myself had witnessed frequently. There were several times in his abrasive company in the latter two years of Waddell's tenure you could tell that alcohol was influencing his conduct. I once found him asleep in a bar in Switzerland when he had travelled with the SFA to an international game. He had been there all night. It was sad to behold. The contrast with the unblemished Wallace could not have been greater. Unknown to the adoring Rangers public he had been hanging on to his own crossbar, for many months in the hope of working something out but could not prevent Waddell's intransigence. And, significantly, Rangers had scored an own goal, as obvious as that floating ball from Ritchie which had deceived McCloy.

39

Breakdown

Scotland v Peru
1–3
World Cup Argentina
3 June 1978
Goal: Joe Jordan

ON THE FLIGHT across the Atlantic the delightful air hostess after pouring us some drinks said to me, 'You know you're representing the whole of the UK.' In her strictly formal cheeriness, I could also recognise a tiny simmer of regret that her own nation, undoubtedly England, since she had a pronounced Birmingham accent, were not flying to Argentina and the World Cup with us, but had been left behind. Since she looked like she was going to be liberal with the drinks trolley I refrained from saying the following so as not to hurt her feelings. 'No, sorry. We are a small nation of only around eight million and many people in the English media think we were damned fortunate to have got through and keep on moaning about how they believe we conned the referee in Liverpool against the Welsh. They'll be sitting hoping we have a disaster. We are on our own, for our own!'

At the same time I knew I had been influenced by some of the English media people I worked with, particularly some Fleet Street connoisseurs of the subtle and brash insult, and not the average guy in the street. But that just happened to be the professional world that influenced my thinking. What I didn't know at the time speaking to her was that my mention of disaster was like I had been tempting providence. For I was about to suffer a personal one on Argentina soil.

Our first game was in the provincial town of Cordoba which now resides in my mind the way Culloden does for my Macpherson clan who were decimated on that moor. The Scottish squad each one of whom was kissed on the cheek by a glamourous senorita for press purposes, on their first day there, which gave rise to wild, baseless rumours of libidinous conduct by some of our gallants, were in fact to be holed up in a crumbling hotel that Hitchcock could have devised for a creepy movie.

But there they were, in front of my eyes warming up on the Cordoba pitch on 3 June 1978 and looking good. Peru looked sort of skinny by comparison, slick, superficial, Billy Bremner-fodder. Who would score our first World Cup finals goal? That was the only thought in my head. Derek Johnstone who had netted 41 goals for Rangers the previous season was left out – the centre-forward position filled by Joe Jordan who had only scored two goals in the last four years for his country. Big decision. Which I could not comment on because an hour before kick-off I was informed the communications line back to Scotland had not been booked in time, so the World Cup authorities had cancelled BBC Scotland's commentary and would insert David Coleman's voice instead. I felt almost like an outcast, or like a man entering the first-night wedding chamber only to discover he was incapable of an erection.

So when our first goal came in a tournament I had been preparing for in the last four years like someone pursuing a PhD, I witnessed it as if through prison bars. Unforgettably. A goal, though, seemed to justify Ally MacLeod's controversial selection because it was Jordan who netted in 14 minutes picking up a rebound off the eccentric keeper Quiroga to slip in a goal from close range in what seemed like a momentous finish, even to my now-crabbit self. For I was still indignant that I was denied describing this, the first Scottish World Cup goal in South America. It haunted me for years. The mood was not helped when Cueto equalised two minutes before half-time. 1–1 Then a man called Teófilo Cubillas changed my attitude. He scored two goals in the space of seven minutes near the end, with a majestic right foot: firstly in a sweeping drive from the edge of the box. Then the classic. The one that any commentator of any nationality would have been proud to describe. It was a front-footed stab of a free kick that I had never seen performed before. There was no stopping it, after which I felt this strong feeling of gratitude that I was actually there to witness greatness in the flesh and, as a bonus, that I was not the carrier of bad news back home of a 1–3 defeat.

40

The Immortal Touch

Scotland v Holland
3–2
World Cup Mendoza
11 June 1978
Goal: Archie Gemmill

FIVE-HUNDRED MILES SOUTH-WEST of Cordoba they grow blissful grapes which produce wine now decorating the shelves of every supermarket on the globe. Back in 1978 the name Mendoza meant nothing to me, for anything, which is why I felt like I had reached football's Shangri La when I stepped into their stadium for the first time. It was as if a gigantic ladle had scooped out a segment of the Andes into a bowl that acted like a paddling pool for some mythical giant from the mountains. It was arguably the most dramatically sited stadium I had ever been in, hemmed in as it was by a string of towering peaks. I was about to watch a game with a Wagnerian back drop and a goal that could have been set to the thrum of the *Ride of the Valkyries*.

The majestic beauty surrounding us did nothing to soothe the depression we felt in having been embarrassed in achieving only a draw against the Iranians in our second game, leaving us with only one point after two games and facing early exit. We were now demob happy. We just wanted out of that damned police state which had attempted to use the tranquillising effect of football as a means of convincing us all was normal. And we were now facing the last task of beating the runners-up in the last World Cup, the Dutch, by three clear goals to stay in the tournament as we saw it at that stage. We were now planning our various bookings for flights back home from Buenos Aires on that prospect.

So, on that June day, the scoring started with the Dutch through a Rensenbrink penalty, in 35 minutes, followed by an equaliser from Kenny Dalglish just on half-time. Scotland looked an improved side though. Graeme Souness in his World Cup debut was making a difference in midfield. Then an Archie Gemmill penalty two minutes into the second half gave us an unexpected 2–1 lead. After which the world was seen in a different hue. For then in the 68th minute came a goal that inspired Renton in the film *Trainspotting* to shout out, 'I haven't felt that good since Archie Gemmill scored against Holland in 1978!' A reasonable analogy since he had just had an orgasm in watching it live on the box, in that particular scene. Myself? Yes, it felt a bit like that on the platform at the time, but later that evening I couldn't get out of my head another image. That of Bruce's successful charge against De Bohun at Bannockburn in June 1314 and how that stole the show. I think it was similar audacity, boldness, leading by example. That blending of images still sticks to this day.

His weaving run, past three defenders executed with remarkable ease, and at pace, to wrong-foot an experienced defender like the great Ruud Krol, through whose legs he poked the ball as if he was a clotheshorse, and then with almost school-boyish impudence merely ushering the ball with his left foot into the net, had a balletic quality. Indeed, I watched a Scottish dance company mimic it years later. And, it inspired Danny Boyle to make that important scene in his *Trainspotting* film, and asking me to re-voice the commentary, with extra passion. Of course, I had no idea it was to supplement Renton's amorous pursuits.

But Gemmill gave us some sense of decency back after so much criticism, heaped upon us mostly because of our pre-World Cup pretensions. Like he was placing his 'plaidie to the angry airt' to take us out of the 'cauld blast'. And, more relevantly, with one more goal we would actually qualify out of the group. That almost euphoric relief lasted only three minutes. There was a sleekit blizzard on stand-by.

Johnny Rep, a Dutchman, scored with indecent haste, hitting a 25-yard shot whose ferocious brilliance simply evoked a sense of injustice. That was it. We were out. The 3–2 victory simply a forlorn statistic. But not the Gemmill goal. For me it remains the Pole Star in the galaxy of goals – permanent, incandescent, but also informing us through cinema that in Mendoza the scoring of a goal had found its rightful place in erotica.

41

Stunning Finale

Celtic v Rangers
4–2
21 May 1979
League title decider
Goal: Murdo MacLeod

EVEN BEFORE A ball was kicked that night I could hardly forget that chat I had with Billy McNeill in the tunnel at Hampden Park, as Aberdeen manager, about to take on Rangers in the Scottish Cup final of 1978. Now, a year later, he was back in what his vast support thought was his natural position, Celtic manager. Although, as we were eventually to discover, not so natural as to be guaranteed longevity. However, the backing he was to get in that game underlined the sudden ache for the past he had felt at Hampden that day.

That Monday was a pleasant spring evening in Glasgow. Rather better than when the game was supposed to have been played on 6 January previously but had been postponed. But other matters in the background were not so comforting. There was a bus and train strike in Glasgow that evening which possibly kept the attendance down to 52,000 when 60,000 had been expected. There was to be no television commentary because of a strike by relevant technicians at the time in the early days of Thatcherism, the lady having come to power only weeks before. So I was installed in the press-box, since having to do a commentary the following weekend at Wembley for the England international I needed the sights of this game to reflect back on, if they were relevant. And, of course they demonstrably were.

It was Celtic's last game of the season, while Rangers had two left. Without going into the possible complications, the bottom line was that Celtic needed to win. A draw would suffice for Rangers. The chips were not only down, but in the atmosphere that night inside Celtic Park you could almost hear them frying. This was the final day of Billy McNeill's first season back at Parkhead, after having left Aberdeen where he and his wife had thoroughly enjoyed living and McNeill had a sound and mutually respectful relationship with the board there and particularly with the affable and understanding chairman Dick Donald. It was his former manager Jock Stein who collared McNeill just after the Aberdeen manager had been presented with the Manager of the Year award at the Macdonald Hotel in Newton Mearns in spring 1978.

McNeill was taken aback when his former manager told him it was time for him to be back at Celtic. At that time Stein, still in charge at Parkhead, was fully aware that some of the Celtic board wanted him out of the club altogether. He was eventually offered a directorship but with an ill-defined brief to increase the club's commercial interests. For a man who had won the club 25 major trophies, the European Cup, the Scottish League Championship ten times, the Scottish Cup eight times and the Scottish League Cup six times, it was a bit like asking Michelangelo to turn his creative mind to tax collection. It was rejected. And McNeill was fully aware that the board at Celtic Park under Desmond White's stewardship would be a different proposition to that at Pittodrie. But he couldn't turn his back on the club with which he had attained greatness.

So while we were all in Argentina attuned to the World Cup we heard that Billy McNeill had been appointed Celtic manager and simultaneously John Greig was now in charge at Ibrox. These two great contemporaries were in the dugouts that May evening at Celtic Park.

Overwhelmingly, when you are reflecting back on a game, you plot your way through a narrative that is logically set out from the first whistle. This day proved to be entirely different. When I start thinking of this game again, I am led firstly and inescapably to that moment in the second half when a Celtic player was sent off. Yes, Rangers had been in the lead by then from a goal by Alex MacDonald in seven minutes and yes, Roy Aitken of Celtic even before that had hit the bar with a header, so you felt a pattern was developing with the team only requiring a draw about to pace the game the way they desired, even with Celtic having the majority of the play. Ten minutes into the second half came the incident. Johnny

Doyle of Celtic was sent off for what the linesman reported to the referee Eddie Pringle from Edinburgh, that he had deliberately kicked the Rangers goalscorer and verified by some of his dismayed teammates afterwards. Down to ten men, and one goal behind, the words I was scribbling in my notetaking could have been construed as an obituary for Celtic.

I could tell from the looks around me in the media area that I was surrounded by like-minded. That did not ease all that much even after Celtic equalised through their captain Roy Aitken in the 66th minute. I recall though the abrupt change in mood around me among the media when George McCluskey with a superb shot put them one up eight minutes later. 2–1. Ten men in the lead? Thinking was changing around me, even when Bobby Russell equalised 2–2 only two minutes later when what looked like a speculative shot through a ruck of players found the net. We were starting to believe almost anything could now happen. No surprise then when under intense pressure Colin Jackson's head deflected a McCluskey shot into the net. 3–2.

The wildly swinging fortunes in this match merited an awesome climax. It had swung so much that the slender lead still looked fragile. What we were to see was stunning. It came from the most expensive player in a Celtic jersey.

Murdo MacLeod's club record transfer fee from Dumbarton of £120,000 was always thought worthy. Now it was to be seen as one of the great inspirational signings made by McNeill. Virtually on the final whistle MacLeod's advance with the ball at his feet towards the Rangers penalty area looked nothing more than simply keeping valuable possession. Until he let blast from 20 yards. The viciously struck sphere was destined for only one place. The top corner of the net. Game won. Title won. 4–2. The MacLeod goal is retained in the mind not just as a spectacle but the effect it had on me and those who write and talk about football for a living. I can guarantee there was not a single one of us who left Celtic Park that night without believing implicitly that Billy McNeill had established himself for life in that role, given the almost incomprehensible nature of a ten-man win. A miracle maker no less. Others in power did not look at life the way we did in penning or voicing our thoughts. When Billy McNeill left the club five years later after having won three Championship titles, and both the Scottish Cup and League Cup, because of disputes over financial matters when effectively a gun was put to his head, and he had to leave, these words appeared in a letter on 7 July that year in the *Glasgow Herald*, from a typical Celtic follower, 'The atmosphere of family has been destroyed, loyalty has been discarded and our spirit of tolerance has been dissipated into a meanness of spirit and servility to money that is deeply abhorrent.'

Reading that and recalling the thrilling MacLeod goal in a night of ecstatic triumph, I don't think I was alone in thinking that Celtic then needed no navigational aid to reach the self-destruct button.

42

Sipping Success

Dundee United v Aberdeen
3–0
Scottish League Cup Final Replay
12 December 1979
Goal: Willie Pettigrew

LIKE JOCK STEIN, Jim McLean was a tea-jenny. If you ever saw them sitting and sipping together as we often did in 1982 in particular, when they were manager and assistant respectively of the national side, and if you weren't any the wiser you could easily take them for a couple of mates just off the bowling-green reminiscing about how elusive the jack had been that day. They exuded the feeling of a quiet understanding of how life can play tricks on you and you just have to get on with it. Those who knew them of course would know that this was as false a picture as believing the Bengal tiger could be a cuddly pet. At their respective heights in the game they were, in different ways, crusaders, armed sometimes with a cudgel called ruthlessness.

I mention the two of them in the same breath for the simple reason that Stein would tell me on several occasions that McLean's achievements were underrated by the vast majority of us south of the Tay whilst at the same time acknowledging that the Dundee United manager had as much a grasp of public relations as Stein had of Swahili. It made an astonishing contrast to be met inside by the genial Mrs Lindsay, the club secretary at Tannadice who would often go out of her way to be helpful, like the times she managed to get me accommodation on the many European nights I enjoyed there. Then Jim McLean would come into the room and make you feel like you had just secretly tunnelled your way in, suspicious, doleful, measuring his words. I always likened him to the old movie star James Cagney, with that brooding toughness straight out of Chicago, not Larkhall, Lanarkshire as was the case. I certainly had a forewarning of his disposition when I played in an invitational golf outing at Gleneagles one blazingly hot day and where I was placed in a foursome with Jim and his brother Willie. The day was as beautiful as the golf was lousy, but even though the weather was glorious, by the end of 18 holes, listening to the pair of them tear down every institution in the land, and particularly the SFA, with a Domesday dourness, I was left wondering if life was worth living after all.

Then when we met for the first time in the football environment, he put me abruptly in my place. It was at Ibrox. In April 1973 half an hour before kick-off I knocked on the Dundee United dressing room door, which was answered by himself and I asked him politely if he could give me his team selection as one normally did as commentator. Out it came, 'If you can give me Jock Wallace's selection I'll give you mine. All you'll do is go and tell him my team. And anyway, I heard what you said about us on the box last night and it was rubbish.' Door slammed in my face.

I admit my egotistical reaction was like, 'Who does he think he is, talking to me like that, this little-known upstart!'

I therefore confess that from that moment in a corridor at Ibrox I realised that any failure on his part would not cause me any pain. At the same time in watching and praising players like Pettigrew, Milne, Sturrock and Bannon, maturing and flourishing under him, I admit he was entirely responsible for their overall style, which was a mix of intelligent use of the ball, with speed an added bonus. Whatever misgivings I had about the personality of McLean, it would have been unprofessional not to acknowledge that something special was brewing inside Tannadice. Even though on 4 May 1976 they went to Ibrox needing at least a draw to avoid relegation, and having to watch their goalkeeper Hamish McAlpine hit the post with a penalty-kick he had taken for the side, I welcomed their survival in achieving a draw. Signs of their transformation were gradually sinking in for a sceptic like myself. The *Sporting Post* commented on United beating Rangers 3–0 for only the second time in nine years on December 1978, '15,247 saw a game that Tannadice fans will tell their grandchildren'.

Yet, even so, I still could not get around to convincing myself that they could win a trophy. That feeling was still there when I was preparing to commentate on United playing Alex Ferguson's Aberdeen in the final of the Scottish League Cup at Hampden on 8 December 1979. Fergie just appeared to have the drive to take on anyone at that stage and gave the impression at times that he judged McLean to be a phenomenon not to treat all that seriously. On one occasion learning that McLean needed a scout for the Glasgow area he phoned him to strongly recommend a man called Lyon and gave him a number to call. The United manager duly phoned and discovered he was talking to the office at Calderpark Zoo.

Revenge was sweet for the United manager. Not at Hampden in the first game, which I recall being particularly nervy played out in front of a miserably low attendance of 27,173 that only deserved the no-scoring draw that followed. No, it was an evening in Dundee, at Dens Park, just down the street from Tannadice the following Wednesday for the replay that history was made. The camera platform we had was under the enclosure roof opposite the main stand. Underneath me was a battalion of Aberdeen supporters who were to offer a rather dramatic opinion later that night.

My choice of Willie Pettigrew's first of two goals in 15 minutes is simply because it offered the first tangible evidence of the transformation that United had undergone. And because in the obvious self-assured control of the game they were exhibiting, there was no way back for Aberdeen. For self-assurance began to ooze out of United. They were discarding parochialism by demonstrating that their corner of the world was the equal of anything that could be produced along the Glasgow–Edinburgh corridor. Pettigrew's presence itself, signed in 1979 from Motherwell, for his striking abilities, was evidence enough of that. He was to score another in the second half, with Paul Sturrock adding a third later to finish the demolition. This provoked the Aberdeen fans underneath us to begin throwing bottles at our platform where not surprisingly they shattered with the glass simply cascading on their own heads.

This was United's first major trophy success and establishing themselves in an amazing era under McLean who was making a visit by teams to Tannadice as appetising as climbing the north face of the Eiger. Under his unique stewardship they were to win the Scottish League Cup twice and above all the Scottish Championship in 1983. From that came considerable European achievements, reaching the semi-final of the European Cup in 1984 and the two-legged UEFA Cup final in 1987 and could proudly claim they are the only club to have beaten Barcelona four times without loss, in different Euro competitions.

But there was a segment in life which still remains elusive. I have Jock Stein to credit for the information. It was about his meeting with McLean in his car in the Hampden car park in 1983 when Stein was then manager of the national side. McLean had asked him for it. Stein, as he put it to me eventually, was not exactly stunned, but nevertheless slightly surprised that he had been asked to make some kind of judgement on the fact that Rangers had been in contact with the United manager to invite him to become their manager to replace John Greig. I wish I had been privy to that conversation between two great footballing brains attempting to reach a conclusion about where the obvious merits would take a man. I have Stein's absolute assurance that having weighed everything up and having recommended he should make the move Jim McLean left his car that day deciding to accept the offer. He was effectively the new Rangers manager. Stein went home and told his wife about the conclusion. Yet, later that night when he turned on the news and heard that McLean in fact had rejected it, Stein's words I recall. 'I felt bloody stupid!' and then added in a whisper to me, 'Cold feet! That's what I think!'

So that first Pettigrew goal which launched the great United period of achievement and created interest in McLean himself leaves us with the daunting, dangling question about that Ibrox offer. What if?

43

Crowded Out

Celtic v Rangers
1–0
10 May 1980
Scottish Cup Final
Goal: George McCluskey

ONCE UPON A time I had a strong impulse to put down the mike and flee for the hills. It was a situation I had not been prepared for, like a man asked to go into the ring and take on Mike Tyson, when all he turned up to do was tell an audience of how good a fighter he was. It was also a day when my relationship with the Glasgow police became ambiguous, according to some of them, who took note of a cry of despair in my voice when broadcasting live on that same day. And I had always prided myself in getting on with the constabulary at football matches since the days I would go to watch Shettleston Juniors and struck up a relationship with a big officer there who came from Skye and I loved listening to that lilting accent which was like a melody by Strauss compared to the guttural sounds which constitute a football crowd. We always thought he was too genial and didn't have a hard streak. But seeing him in action once when there was some trouble outside the ground, like heaving a man off his feet with a technique that must have been acquired in the sheep-fields of his island home, not police training college, I developed an everlasting respect for the constabulary from that single officer. Or I thought I had.

But consider what broadcaster and writer Tom English wrote about my relationship with the police in the *Scotsman* of 2010, reflecting on that infamous day 10 May 1980 when the Hampden Park pitch was covered by hundreds of football supporters engaged in clashes that would cause serious injury to many and besmirch Scottish football. His words were uncompromising.

'If Chief Inspector Ian McKie could have heard the commentary on that May day at Hampden 30 years ago he might well have left his position on the pitch, left the rampaging Old Firm supporters, left the cans and the bricks, left the worst outbreak of hooliganism in Scotland in 70 years, and marched straight up to where Archie Macpherson was sitting, microphone in hand, and throttled him live on the air.'

Why? Because of my imploring words it seems.

'They're spilling right on to the pitch,' Archie was saying, 'And where are the police? For heaven's sake, where are the police?'

English, to his credit, acknowledges that McKie had after-thoughts and the writer expressed them thus, 'McKie thinks back now and says in fairness to Archie, he called it right.'

Before I would claim immunity from any blame that day, I have to confess I was far from flawless. I was also a victim in a curious way which still haunts me. It was said immediately afterwards that a single winning goal ignited the fire. But that day, hanging over Hampden, was an even bleaker element to add to the normal animosities in Glasgow, because of factors elsewhere. Many in the Glasgow police with experience of those fixtures and their fractious aftermaths, sniffed danger. One in particular was Colin Weir who was then sergeant in the division of the police which supervised Hampden on match days. He summed up to me what the broad consensus view of police in the city was about the coming Saturday.

'Anybody who knew anything about Scottish football knew that with one of those teams likely to end the season with nothing then somewhere there would be trouble. But at that time, out of the blue came the word that the presence of the police at the stadium was to be hugely decreased. It originated from the city fathers saying, 'We're not going to pay all this money.' We knew what we were going to need to police this huge event particularly in these special circumstances. On the Friday before the event our divisional commander went up to headquarters and actually begged to have more bodies on duty. Nothing doing. Normally the police inside the stadium would leave about ten minutes from the end to attend to the departure of fans. So, even with depleted numbers inside that day, they did exactly that. They left.'

The special circumstances that Colin was referring to was the fact that

Aberdeen had won the league the previous Saturday at Easter Road and Dundee United had lifted the Scottish League Cup earlier in the season, which meant that either Celtic or Rangers would end the season with nothing to brag about, for the coming year, or even years it could be said. To some it would feel like being disembowelled, both factions being fully aware that in pubs, offices and workbenches throughout the land they would be subject to painful reminders of a special defeat, and by whom, with no riposte to hand. This added fuel to their already existing passion, and desperation to win.

Now I had never been conscious of the policing of a major event inside Hampden, and as usual I was engrossed in trying to make something of this game which was turning out to be influenced by the fear of defeat, which seemed to me more acute than it ever had been in past meetings. Yes, there were one or two reasonable opportunities in the game but overall, I recall being disappointed that there was to be extra-time given the mediocrity of the event. Celtic scored the only goal of the game in the 107th minute and thereafter I was submerged in commentating on a crowd invasion, started by Celtic fans, aided by the fact that PC Tom McLeod, a self-confessed Rangers supporter, for the sake of safety and not wanting another Hillsborough, opened the gates in the fence to help relieve pressure at that end. As night follows day on came the Rangers support and battle commenced. What eventually transpired made me think, at the end of it, of that old music-hall crack, 'And what did you think of the play, Mrs Lincoln?' as I realised these scenes would be transmitted throughout the world and plaster the front pages of every newspaper in our land, and well beyond, leaving the football match behind as a limp postscript.

Naturally we kept the cameras running to cover cup presentation etc and the blarney interviews that follow. And normally another presenter at pitch-side would take over with scene-sets and interviews. But with the serried ranks now merging into a chaotic morass in the middle of the pitch with missiles being thrown repeatedly and making Hampden look like it was midge-infested, fans being kicked and stamped on and the Red Cross volunteers dealing with the first casualties, my whole feeling was that I wanted nothing to do with it. However, the producer decided to stay with me. There is such a thing as continuity of commentating and I was bound by it. And this was certainly not my scene. The only controversies I ever had to contend with were about dubious off-sides, controversial sendings-off, barmy refereeing and the SFA, which was an institution always seemingly worthy of a poke or two. And I was well-armed with countless cliches to handle these situations and sometimes actually enjoyed doing so. We had no VAR in those days of course when I had the freedom to make judgements that would either reflect my brilliance or reveal me as a clown. A situation I believe the modern TV commentator would look back at with affection.

But within about five minutes of the really serious clashes starting, paradoxically I began to feel almost thankful that I could get my teeth into comments that had a distinctive edge to them after the banalities of the game itself. I suddenly found analogies coming to my lips. They came just as naturally as a burp or a sneeze without any pre-thought. Out came a reference to the First World War and the battlefield of Passchendaele. Then reaching my lips was the mention of a highly popular film depicting the Vietnam horrors named *Apocalypse Now*. Even I am surprised they shoved their way in before Bannockburn or El Alamein. And I have to admit that had the white horses not intervened and put an end to the affair, but had warring fans instead devasted the whole stadium and moved out into the streets with the same belligerence, then, by the comparisons I had already made who is to say I would not have given that single bomb in Hiroshima a mention.

I was totally absorbed in the comments but at the same time unsure of myself, as the game itself seemed to have evaporated for me. So why is that Celtic goal included in my overall selection, given I felt the game had been minimised by events? It was because of what happened next. As I left my commentary position after hours sitting there, I was certainly concerned about how I had handled the riot. Had I been over-the-top with the historical references? Was it right to be outspoken about the absence of the police and in the way I expressed it, when clearly it was the strategy that was at fault and whoever was directly responsible for it? I was perplexed. In that febrile state of mind a fan, near the bottom of the stairs near the exit threw a question at me.

'Archie, what did ye think o' that bloody game? Who was your star man?'

I can't remember my exact reply but fobbed it off with some banter concluding with a plea that I desperately needed a pee. For I had to admit to myself with something approaching a shiver that I could not recall anything about the game other than the Celtic goal. The riot instead was running through me like a purgative for the football itself. Definitely for the first time in my career I could not have faced a camera and given a valid account of the game's narrative which took 107 minutes to resolve. The game had gone. The goal stood out like finding a nugget on a coal bing. Not for its excellence, but because it had not vanished underneath the debris of the riot. It came from sleight of foot, meaning, Danny McGrain, who should have scored many more goals in his career to take the advantage of his great attacking skills, takes a shot at goal. It is going well-wide until Celtic striker George McCluskey with his back to goal almost, reaches out his foot to divert the ball away from the Girvan Lighthouse, Peter McCloy in the Rangers goal, and finds the net. That winning goal was greeted with both joy, and I suspect with some relief, by the Celtic support although we are left to ponder if it was a goal by design or a fluke.

Of course, it cannot stand against the competing images of the day, the sunniest of which was the charge of the white horses that solved the issue. And I now know, in reflection, that the specific emotion I felt watching the triumph of their action was exactly how I felt when I saw the Shettleston officer from Skye exercising his uniformed authority in that ruckus back in the old days. It's called pride.

44

A Likely Lad

Celtic v Rangers
3–1
Scottish League
21 February 1981
Goal: Charlie Nicholas

STRIKERS MEANT A lot to me. They raised the pulse rate and stretched the larynx in paroxysms of emotion that ranged from anguish to celebration. I still think my reaction to the Kenny Dalglish goal at Anfield in the World Cup qualifier against Wales in 1977 took me to heights I never thought the human voice could ever reach, for instance. And there is no doubt I assessed strikers differently from other players. They put you on edge. An air of suspense inevitably followed the good ones. You never knew what exactly to anticipate even when commenting on somebody with a credible reputation in front of goal.

I believe this perplexity stemmed from an incident when I was a schoolboy. I had managed to be provided with a ticket for the Scotland–England game at Hampden in 1950 in the schoolboys' enclosure, low down at the front of the old south-east stand. That enclosure was a cauldron of vituperative anti-English sloganising which perhaps would not have gone down well with some of their social studies teachers back in the classroom. But we all wanted Scotland to go to Rio and take part in the World Cup and the SFA had stated that if we did not lose the game they would head for the Sugar-Loaf mountain in those days when such openness existed. A draw would do. They could have gone anyway, but they put that condition on themselves for reasons that are still baffling.

Not surprisingly we wanted more than a draw and were giving youthful hysterical encouragement that never faltered even though England had taken the lead 1–0 and were holding on grimly towards the end of the game.

Our centre-forward that day was the Hearts player Willie Bauld who had come into this game with a solid reputation. I cannot recall exactly when his moment for potential glory came but it was near the final whistle. The English defence had been agonisingly solid. But on this occasion Bauld found a freedom just outside the six-yard line. He had his side to goal and I still can see the face looking down at the ball which had popped up neatly in front of him just below waist height. Perfect. The schoolboys' enclosure uniformly stretched to tiptoe, like altogether we were tightening our genitals in expectation. Bauld struck. Given the strength of the shot I will always recall the way the ball rebounded from the crossbar and almost cleared the penalty area.

That miss haunted me for as long as I can recall, almost like a death in the family given we had invested so emotionally in a Scotland appearance in South America. So that role of being the principal provider of goals I view with that special association. I have seen a budding Bauld in every other striker I have commented on knowing how fine a line there is to be drawn between success and failure and the part these men play in determining enjoyment or despair for whoever follows them. Fortunately in my time in Scottish football I had the privilege of describing the actions of two men in particular who had me properly on edge on many an occasion with alacrity and a sunny disposition to life in general which you could identify even out there on the field. They were Charlie Nicholas and Ally McCoist. I actually grew fond of both largely because I described so many of their goals and near misses and they were never short of comment either when you put them in front of a camera. They, in fact, racked up 375 goals between them for the Old Firm, the bulk of which were claimed by Ally because of his greater number of his appearances. Their stories parallel each other in many ways but crucially different in other areas. Take Charlie first.

I recall travelling to Celtic Park that day in 1981 through the centre of Glasgow which was dominated by a trade union demonstration, 50,000 strong to protest against the Tory government and reminding us that our love of the game might blind us to the realities of life. Inside a packed Celtic Park though the insulation provided by the hate-fest made that street life seem of another world. Now I had heard promising things about Charlie but kept in mind that he was a teenager and could be susceptible to the unique pressures of that fixture. Not only that, in my introduction as the teams ran out I was reminding the audience of the apparent Celtic dilemma. Rangers had won the first derby 3–0. Both Aberdeen and Dundee United were threatening the Glasgow duopoly and in the December before this game Celtic had lost heavily to Fergie's Aberdeen 4–1. This was asking a great deal of the current Celtic side but particularly of a largely raw teenager.

This game, with snow falling occasionally was really about a Celtic revival and a storming second-half performance that made Rangers, in the biting cold, seem peely-wally. Yes, they had gone into the lead in only 11 minutes from a subtle header by Derek Johnstone again, no less, whom you have thought would have been under defensive padlock given his reputation. After which came the moment that I commentated on my first Charlie goal. It came in 57 minutes when it looked like it was one of those days when Celtic could play till midnight without making a breakthrough. Rangers had been packing their penalty area and shot after shot rebounded off bodies and legs. In one of those assaults a ball rebounded to the feet of the teenager who in tight space swept it past McCloy in the Rangers goal. It was a shot of alertness, of being present in the right space at the right time. That predatory instinct of perception amongst a crowd of bodies was evidence of clear-headedness. Not spectacular, but telling, because it broke the Rangers dam. That goal in particular put him centre-stage in my mind. Charlie did score again with a similar kind of goal and Roy Aitken added a third for a deserved Celtic 3–1 victory that owed much to the teenager. Now I never reflect on that his first ever goal against Rangers, and the first Charlie goal for me, without considering the consequences which flowed from it. For there and then he had stamped on himself an irrevocable Celtic identity. He was paying his dues already to the club he always had wanted to play for. He was clearly a 'lifer'. Or so I implicitly believed, as did many others.

Afterwards Billy McNeill was predictably bullish in front of camera but rambled somewhat as he praised his young star to me. But to the press he was more studied, and in his statement afterwards there was a hint of what was to come for the 'lifer'. He told them, 'When Charlie was 16 he played in a youth tournament after which one English club offered us £70,000 for him. Of course it was turned down for even then it was obvious the lad was a bit special. The world is going to hear a lot more about Charlie.' A sincere endorsement for new quality at Celtic Park, but with the revelation that there was wide interest in the new star. But he was Celtic through and through. Which is why I could scarcely believe my ears when I heard that on the 22 June 1983 he had been transferred to Arsenal after having scored 48 goals in 74 appearances for a club he would have crawled over broken glass to play for.

Just before that transaction I sat beside Billy McNeill at a charity dinner when, because of the bond we had struck up when he had assisted me in the World Cup in Spain he was astonishingly frank with me about his relationships with certain people on the Celtic board. He was clearly a deeply unhappy man and the selling of Charlie against his wishes simply broke his back and he departed south. Nicholas and McNeill, both departed, was – without addressing the financial aspects of the event, as a classic act of self-hurt by the club – aggravated for me by hearing of Charlie's London lifestyle where the moniker Champagne Charlie was pinned to him. What's more, I missed him in games. He always had the potential to exercise my vocal chords. But there was no absolute vacuum for me as Ally was still there wedded to a club, despite ups and downs and in manner, as we shall see later, that was a model of fidelity that somehow Celtic had overlooked about their own wonderful finisher.

45

The Tartan Rebirth

Scotland v Brazil
1–4
World Cup
18 June 1982
Goal: David Narey

EVEN BEFORE A ball was kicked in the Estadio Benito Villamarin. Even before a memorable goal was scored. Even before an iconic English football analyst tried to demean that goal, the city of Seville in June 1982, presented us with something historic occurring in front of our eyes. For it is my belief that the streets of that city gave birth to what we now call the Tartan Army. Watching the longest conga-line ever seen anywhere in the world, comprising of both Scottish and Brazilian supporters winding its way through the city squares with almost brotherly love and in a spirit of carnival, made a dramatic contrast to the dumb triumphalism of Ally's Army of the immediate past, and the grim wreckers in tartan whom I had witnessed altering some of the architecture of London on Wembley visits. The midwifery for this came from the notorious new reputation of the English supporters themselves who were now acting like Viking raiders anywhere they visited. The Scottish fans, fully aware of that, were being re-born!

All this was dramatically obvious to myself and co-commentator Billy McNeill, the former Celtic player and manager, as we had just left a man who had openly raised his eyes to the heavens and almost uttered a prayer that the Scots would behave themselves in that lovely city. He was Sean Connery, sitting sipping tea with us, poolside, in Toni Dalli's restaurant in Puerto Banus, just outside Marbella. Credit to McNeill for suggesting in the first place that the most famous Scot in the world would provide a colourful endorsement of our lads, just after the scare we had against New Zealand in our opening World Cup game. Yes, Scotland had won, but with a characteristic lapse in concentration which had the score at 3–2 at one stage, but ending more comfortably 5–2. Our professional cameramen, recording this interview for *Grandstand* were not distracted by the topless lady sunning herself in the pool nearby, and 007 delivered us some comfortable nostrums about how Scotland seemed to perform better against stronger nations, yes, like Brazil. I could have challenged him on that statistic but wanted to keep him on our side. This ex-Hib rookie, who if he had played well enough and been a success on the field, could have had a sumptuous alternative career, and ended up owning a pub near Easter Road, was simply a typical Scottish supporter who was actually in the dark, like ourselves, about how we might survive, or perhaps even thrive on that particular day. He was clearly part of the football family who was emotionally tied to our performances, and not some remote unconcerned icon. That's all we wanted from him, for it was important to indicate to some English sceptics the emotional strength and diversity of the Scottish footballing family.

The one man we had in mind was Jimmy Hill, the principal English football analyst of the age, whom McNeill and I had dinner with the day before the game and during which the long-chinned fellow complained about not having received a knighthood in the recent honour's list published. It struck us also that he was little informed about the Scottish squad, and in a charitable mood the former Celtic captain filled him in with some essential details. So we were immediately wary of him. Smooth talking, utterly self-confident and obviously not all that concerned that he was going to be presenting half-time and full-time analysis on the game in Seville, given his lack of current information about the Scots. But he was the last of our thoughts, as we settled into our commentary positions, and had to cope with the first impressions of the Brazilians on the field warming up.

They always look like they have no equal. Lithe, supple, with ball control that looks like they are circus performers on the side, and with the heritage of the great Pele still attached to them, McNeill and I felt the customary sensation of simply being honoured to be present to see a Scottish side on the same field as them. With it came the hope that this sense of awe would evaporate at kick-off, as it did. And McNeill and I had covered the Brazil–Russia first match, during which we had to stop talking to allow a BBC announcer to tell the audience that the war in the Falklands was now officially over. But the other remarkable fact was that Brazil looked clever on the ball but could only win 2–1 a couple of minutes from time from a 20-yard screamer by Eder. They simply looked too leisurely at times. So we began commentary not without hope.

No Danny McGrain on the field, who had made the kind of mistake in the first game that Stein was perhaps acknowledging that this great player was past his best. Notably a relatively inexperienced player at this level took his place. David Narey. I recall saying, early on, with great authority, that Narey would hardly move from a defensive position. Yes, of course, the Brazilians were pinging the ball about like they were about to put on an exhibition with Socrates, the captain, at the fulcrum, and the running of Oscar, Cerezo and Zico, around him with the ball seemingly glued to their feet was impressive – but without really causing any bother to Alan Rough in goal who had no save to make in the first 15 minutes.

Then it came. With little warning. Like it was cocking-a-snoot at the glamorous façade of artistic football encapsulating the pitch. Even years later and before the dementia had sadly weakened his mind Billy McNeill and I would look back and recount the 18th minute of that game, like we had had a vision of something unearthly that we alone had witnessed. It was never anything other than 'our goal'.

Souness flighting a ball forward found the head of John Wark who headed it into the path of David Narey who having fled his defensive position put boot to ball from the edge of the penalty area. As it rocketed to the net I think incredulity was present in my mind before I reacted. We were one up against Brazil. That was a fact. An exhilarating fact that we clutched on to for a meagre 15 minutes.

Yes, Zico equalised for Brazil, but at half-time with the score 1–1 McNeill and I settled in to purr over the audacity of this relatively unknown Scottish player. Then wearing our earphones we heard Jimmy Hill's half-time summary. He was perched on a platform on the roof of a high-rise apartment block, overlooking the ground. From our position we could look up and both hear and see his pontificating. Billy McNeill was sipping a glass of water (almost 100 degrees had been registered in the stadium) when Hill mentioned the Narey goal. When he then used the words 'toe-poke' to describe it with a kind of nonchalance as if it had been a fluke, accidentally produced by an amateur, my co-commentator spluttered the water over both himself and me. He was enraged. Immediately he had clocked the fact that Hill was in a Brazilian trance, flavoured by English insensitivity.

When the Brazilians really showed their brilliance in the second-half and ran over us with added goals by Oscar, Eder and Falcao for 4–1, I admit that it took the heat out of our immediate response to the 'toe-poke' jibe. They were simply a great team, although their arrogance that was evident in both games we had covered was, sadly, to prove their downfall against the ruthlessly practical Italians later in the competition. What we did ensure was that our journalistic colleagues knew what Hill had said, knowing full well that it would go down as well with them as calling haggis dogfood. We never did come across him again in the tournament. And throughout Seville that night Scots began to appreciate, even in defeat, how fortunate we were to be rubbing shoulders with the aristocracy of the game that at one stage had been 'sair affronted' by a Scottish foot, toes and all.

46

That Memorable Hug

Aberdeen v Real Madrid
2–1
European Cup Winners Final
11 May 1983
Goal; John Hewitt

WINNING TWO MAJOR cup finals in the space of two weeks gave Alex Ferguson the look of a new impresario in the land who had mastered all the techniques of his particular business and would be pulling in plentiful customers for the rest of his life. Even without knowing what future lay in front of him I did feel he would never end up in pensionable age at Pittodrie. He would move on. You only needed to sit with him talking fervently and frequently in that boot room in the stadium, particularly in his run to win the European Cup Winner's Cup in season 1982/3, to appreciate a man with an ambition to scale the heights that would not be fully satisfied so close to the North Sea. His stature rose in front of my eyes as I kind of clung on to Aberdeen's back on their sorties on the continent that season. When I watched them beat Bayern in the quarter-finals I sensed that greatness was his in the making. Then came two finals in the space of two weeks that produced two goals that merit special consideration for the way they played with my emotions.

For some goals have odd consequences even for those who triumph on the back of them. That May day goal I have singled out at Hampden is now firmly in that curious category for that very reason, despite being overshadowed by Aberdeen goals earlier in that week. It produced a unique reaction in a now notorious interview on the track at the end of a very long afternoon, which had begun to look like a cup final replay had been pre-ordained. As for its special pedigree, firstly, the man who scored the winner in that Hampden final, Eric Black, was a European Champion no less. He had returned with his colleagues helping to carry the European Cup Winners trophy from Gothenburg, Aberdeen having beaten one of the great names in football, Real Madrid, 2–1 a few days before. Glasgow though would be a more hostile arena than they had experienced in the Swedish stadium, with Rangers being their opponents. Although they were to experience a quite unique hostility that some who wore red for Ferguson cannot comprehend to this day.

My problem with Aberdeen reaching Gothenburg and the Nya Ullevi stadium for the final was that it seemed highly likely that I would not get there myself. The game had been allocated to the BBC's rivals ITV as per alternating agreements. Since I had been fortunate enough to have been in both Lisbon and Barcelona covering the last two Scottish successful European finals I felt highly indignant that I would not make it a treble. At that stage of my life I was working principally in London at BBC Television Centre, while travelling back at weekends for commentary work on the Scottish game. So based among English broadcasters who really only believed two Scottish clubs were worth concerning themselves about, I knew it might be difficult to convince them to send me to Sweden, merely to report on a game or to do interviews, while ITV had the rights to cover the game itself. BBC London could have used a locally based reporter with ease. But I always had an ally in the news department in London. Frank Bough I had known for years, as a presenter for sports in a variety of roles, but principally as the established voice for their main show *Grandstand*. He knew me well and he knew his football thoroughly, having commentated on the famous North Korean victory over Italy in the 1966 World Cup game at Middlesborough, but now was in a general news role. I also knew he was deeply unpopular with his female co-presenters who felt they were treated like objects by him and later he was sacked by the BBC in 1988 for revelations about his indiscreet and highly colourful sex life. But he was my mate and I believe he played a part in convincing the editor that I should be there to watch a Scottish team in a European final. The job would be straightforward, simply to report and then interview whoever was available, regardless of result.

In the couple of days before the final I spent some time with the Aberdeen squad at their training camp, and with Jock Stein, the victor in the European

Cup in 1967 of course, wandering the precincts as a guest of the club, you could tell that Alex Ferguson was trying to create a sense of an impending historic challenge for his players and that anything was possible as Stein had demonstrated in a previous year. Willie Miller, his captain, also noticed a change in his manager when he told me, 'He was exceptionally calm. Normally he had this nervous cough when the stress was on particularly before big games. Sometimes it was so intense you felt he was going to vomit. But he just seemed to be enjoying the whole idea of being there.'

Then it rained. It never seemed to stop from the day of getting up in the morning of the game to the kick-off. The pitch looked heavy and would scar easily you could tell. And unlike Lisbon and Barcelona the occasion was seeming to fail to match the standards of a European final, ie glorious sunshine and a pitch like a bowling-green. Indeed it had the definite appearance of a Scottish Cup game in early December, although with levels of skill that reminded you pointedly of what footballing heights you were watching. And it was Eric Black who deservedly put his side into the lead in only seven minutes on the gluey surface and you could tell Real were offended by both the climate in Sweden and the impudence of this club from the north-east of Scotland treating them with apparent ease. Of course, the Spaniards equalised. It was from the penalty spot when Leighton the Aberdeen keeper was judged by the referee to have brought down the speedy Santillana. Juanito scored, with the suggestion that the real Real would now emerge. They didn't. John Hewitt's diving, headed spectacular winner in extra-time, having come on for Black, made it irrevocably 2–1 in the 112th minute. After the final whistle came the hug, that I can still feel even as I type the word. From my low observer's position just behind the Aberdeen dugout I was first to reach the overjoyed Ferguson on the pitch and we exchanged a leaping, almost aerial balletic hug that contrasts vividly with the clash we had months later which prompted a police intervention.

Breakfast Time was pleased with my report given they had covered a 'British' triumph. And in some comfort I prepared for that next final at Hampden believing that nothing could have as big an impact on me as that Hewitt European winner. Life indeed does play strange tricks on you because it was to be overshadowed by what happened at Hampden ten days later. That Hewitt goal I always associate with the success that took him and his players to another final and an interview that would bring them back to earth with a galactic bump.

47

Withering Words

Aberdeen v Rangers
(after extra-time)
Scottish Cup Final
21 May 1983
Goal: Eric Black

THE SCOTTISH CUP final only ten days after the Gothenburg triumph was like a homecoming that required a kind of proof of identity. If you are European victors, go ahead and show us these credentials. That was the kind of mood among the media who certainly did not expect a walkover by the Dons. Nor was it to be. At that stage in life I could justifiably claim to be close to Fergie. After all he had organised the Aberdeen Supporters Association to present me with a rose-bowl for the intimacy I had developed with the club during their European run. For we had spent hours in the boot room at Pittodrie gossiping about the game, the events, its personalities, which he loved, as if I were a useful outlet to an outside world which he felt still did not take Aberdeen seriously enough. I recall the day he vividly recounted to me the inducement of the Rangers chairman John Paton to return to Ibrox as manager, but which he treated with contempt for family reasons and because he had never forgotten the club's negative reaction to him, indeed had shown him the door, after he was accused of not covering Billy McNeill in the 1969 Scottish Cup final for an opening goal which led to a rout. I admit though, he made it for me perhaps my most stimulating period in football. I was never closer to any other manager. There are matters we discussed which remain private to this day.

Rangers in that period were managed by the iconic John Greig. He had statistics to his name which were staggering by comparison with others in the game. You have to take a deep breath before you address them. Seven-hundred and fifty-five official appearances for the club, 72 in the Scottish Cup, a club record of 121 in the League Cup and 64 in European tournaments, scoring 120 goals in the winning also of three domestic trebles and that European trophy. It's not the stats I keep recalling about John. It is his character. He was an immense figure when you relate him to the problems Rangers had to face throughout his captaincy. There was the Ibrox disaster when 66 fans were killed on staircase 13 and the club's dignity was personified by both John and the manager Willie Waddell in the aftermath by working among the support to emphasise that the club was a social unit with a bond that even such a tragedy could not disrupt and perhaps make even stronger. There was the Celtic superiority around the early 1970s when Rangers would have collapsed without him on the field. In an Old Firm game played at Hampden on 16 September 1972, because of renovation work being undertaken on a stand at Parkhead, Celtic were so superior and winning by three goals through Dalglish, Johnston and Macari, that when John scored a goal for Rangers in the very last minute, it was greeted by ironic cheers from the Celtic end. It was not spoofing John. It was Rangers they meant. He raised his hand to them in acknowledgement of an opposing support who knew full well his worth to his club.

And in Barcelona when some Rangers players were coming to me asking, 'What do you think they're going to do to us?' meaning UEFA, on the back of the ensuing riot John was using that brilliant wit of his, not to underrate the consequences, but to steady the ship, take minds off any potential penalties. Would all of that provide an insurance policy for a man moving from outstanding player to management?

It never is. He never really bridged it the way many, even in the media, including myself, thought he would. Yes, there were isolated achievements but in the League Championship he could never lift his club to the top. Not surprisingly it affected him. The sharp wit which always prefaced our conversations turned into doubt, mistrust, aggression. Near the tail end of that season in 1983 Aberdeen came to Ibrox and scored two quick goals in the second half. Ibrox began to empty. In commentary I used the phrase, 'The fans are voting with their feet.' I was confident enough in declaring that because you didn't need to put your ear to the ground to know that the once-adoring fans had turned against this icon. As a result of these commentating words he banned me from talking to his players again that season. Such a deterioration in relationships in the game was hardly uncommon. So although nobody was openly billing this cup final as Greig's last chance to redeem himself, it was now a virulent undercurrent of chat among even his most loyal admirers.

I recall feeling that this Scottish Cup final was too long. It was a drawn-out affair suffused with the fear of defeat influencing both sides.

Yes, the game had its moments when a breakthrough seemed likely, but on the other hand as the minutes passed the stalemate looked almost pre-ordained. The Aberdeen goal, though, four minutes from the end of extra-time elicited from me as commentator the simple and colossally obvious statement that the cup was now won, even with time left. The headed goal by young Eric Black in the 116th minute from a deflected cross was clearly a stake driven through the heart of the Rangers psyche. You could almost hear ramparts collapsing. And on the final whistle I came down from that high commentary position looking forward to an interview pitch-side with a manager who now looked as if he could be the colossus of a new age. Which is why I almost dropped the microphone when in his first comment to me in front of camera he uttered a bitter criticism of some of the play he had witnessed. I thought he was referring to Rangers at first. Then it became eminently clear he was talking about his own team, who having just won a second cup had apparently let him down with the standard of football they had played. He was scathing of his own players and only exempted Willie Miller and Alex McLeish, his central defenders, from this astounding attack. I tried to divert him into a more objective analysis of the game and towards appreciation of the victory. He was having none of it. His mind was made up, as Peter Weir, his outstanding winger, confirmed to me years later.

'We were all celebrating in the dressing room and the champagne was popping. We weren't aware of what he had said on camera and then he came in. He went crazy. He shouted for us all to sit down, and then went ballistic, saying things you couldn't repeat now.'

It was only months later when I was subjected to similar treatment by the same man that I was forced to reassess my own rather naïve ideas of the reliability of relationships in this unpredictable sport. He was to launch a verbal attack on me prior to a Hibernian–Aberdeen match at Easter Road for having criticised his goalkeeper Jim Leighton, that blew away the cosy feeling that I was actually a friend of his who had felt a special bond with him after that hug in Gothenburg. The obscenities that we both resorted to in that loud altercation in front of astonished witnesses, provoked an inspector of the Edinburgh constabulary to intervene with a warning of action about to be taken by him, if we didn't desist. From afar I then watched his spectacular successes with Manchester United and began to think that this unique personality was governed by deep emotions that us mere mortals find difficult to comprehend and that surviving the screaming side of this man's spiritual drive, is something we ought to boast about like a war-veteran his scars. I try to comfort myself with that thought, as I also acknowledge of how that Eric Black goal at Hampden was to reveal the ruthless nature of a driven man for whom conventional boundaries simply didn't exist.

48

The Saddest Night

Wales v Scotland
0–1
World Cup qualifier
10 September 1985
Goal: Davie Cooper

JOCK STEIN ONCE watched a goal that confirmed his long admiration for a particular player. It was on August 4 1979 in the Drybrough Cup final.

Now whatever anybody else thought, as a broadcaster I found it difficult to take the Drybrough Cup too seriously. A cup final in August seemed to us like we were being asked to cover a wedding rehearsal rather than the actual wedding ceremony itself later in the year. I recall travelling with an entire Outside Broadcast Unit to Hampden on these August occasions like we were all stiff in the joints and not really up to speed to take on any major clash. And as a commentator I wondered about cup final hyperbole so early in the season. At the best of times you could sound over-the-top. With this short tournament occurring so soon, you could easily find yourself lapsing into falsetto. I felt withdrawn and rather aloof from these games but went through them mechanically knowing that the real stuff was swiftly to follow.

Then, of course, there were moments in these finals that you could scarcely forget. Like that sun-drenched afternoon only months after Stein had been appointed Scotland manager, after his brief sojourn at Leeds. It was an Old Firm final which unavoidably adds a special dimension to any competition. In my commentary I reflected on how Rangers were the superior side inspired by a goal by Sandy Jardine who, running from his own penalty area, into Celtic's, scored perhaps the best goal of his career. But that was nothing compared to what was to follow. By comparison a delicacy was served up. With the score 2–0 Davie Cooper picked up a pass on the edge of the Celtic penalty area and with a sequence of touches that kept the ball in the air, and at the same time flicking it over the heads of several defenders in a 'keepie-uppie' motion, he finally slipped it past the keeper with a Brazilian nonchalance. Some would claim it as the best individual Rangers goal ever.

But the Brazilian analogy is the very one Stein uttered to me when I was chatting to him, a whole four years later in 1985 when he quoted that very goal to me in discussing his squad for the make-or-break confrontation with the Welsh in Cardiff, in the World Cup group game. He valued Cooper's inspirational technique that was '…in his bones like the Brazilians', he said. In other words the Rangers left-winger possessed something of the unorthodoxy that any manager could value and was an automatic selection for the squad, even though he could be notoriously unpredictable. The skill was always on hand though, latent, huffy. He also could take penalties.

What I also noted in that conversation with Stein and in his final press conference before leaving with his team for Cardiff was how drawn and pale he looked. The previous World Cup in Spain had drained him greatly and now at 63 he could not disguise the fact that like anybody else he was vulnerable. I was on BBC news duty that night in Cardiff as the game was ITV's. The plan was simply for me to report live from Cardiff the morning after the game for *Breakfast Time*, regardless of the outcome. I had also accepted an invite to speak at a dinner for a variety of Welsh and Scottish businessmen in Cardiff Castle, immediately after the game.

I was not entirely surprised that Cooper was on the bench at kick-off. That he would play a part at some juncture I felt was not in any doubt. Now when I am not actively participating in a match with Scotland I am truly on edge and sitting watching Mark Hughes scoring for the Welsh in 13 minutes, putting the ball through Willie Miller's legs and past Jim Leighton in goal to be one up, I was painfully aware that Scotland at that stage were out of the World Cup. Alan Rough then having to come on to replace Leighton because the goalkeeper had lost his contact lenses, added to the feeling of disorientation. I wanted to broadcast and offer some words of encouragement. Instead, well into the second half I was feeling like a helpless witness to a car crash. When Cooper eventually came on to replace Strachan after 61 minutes I still felt the situation was getting beyond our grasp.

To this day I wonder how I would have felt if Scotland had given away a penalty in the manner the Welsh did. A David Speedie shot hit Welsh defender Phillips' arm. To the consternation of the Welsh the Dutch referee Keizer awarded a penalty with only nine minutes remaining. I felt such an enormous sense of gratitude to the referee and his judgement in that specific instance that I really was not moved by the sense of injustice that prevailed around me in centre-stand. Still the penalty had yet to be converted. I watched Cooper place the ball on the spot then look calmly at the goal. This was not really about the rare skill he possessed but about nerve most of all. Still, I couldn't get the Drybrough Cup final goal out of my mind as he made his first movement towards the ball.

To be honest, it was not a well-taken penalty. He did not disguise it properly. And it was low to the side of Neville Southall in goal who almost got a hand to it. But it slipped past him and holding on to that 1–1 score I rose from my seat as the final whistle went, with a World Cup spriteliness surging through me. But I had to rush off to fulfil that after-dinner speaking engagement at Cardiff Castle, although on the way somebody in the crowd, recognising me, shouted out, 'Is big Jock all right!' I had no idea what he was talking about and rushed on thinking of how to balance my account of the game and its consequences, to an audience of split loyalties and on the back of a controversial penalty decider.

It was not until we had been served the soup course at the dinner that I was made aware of the tragic scene I had left behind, when Duncan Revie, the son of the great English football manager Don Revie, and organiser of the castle event, whispered in my ear, 'My dad's been on the phone. Jock died just after the game. He doesn't know the details. Would you let the guests know?' He had to repeat these words, more pointedly, before I could grasp what he had just told me. I managed to struggle out a tribute to Stein to a solemn audience without knowing any details of what had occurred.

My long-time researcher Pat Woods was at that game as well. He had split loyalties having been born in Bangor in North Wales, with a Welsh mother. After the game he went for a drink with a friend. Still stunned at having then heard of the passing of his idol, the night took another odd turn. For a man came in later and sat beside them and in friendly but muted conversation they actually started to talk about the game itself.

Astonishingly, this man with the heavy Dutch accent turned out to be the referee of the night's game, Jan Keizer. Pat, a football purist, if ever there was one, made the comment to him that he felt the penalty awarded to Scotland was a mistake. There was no turmoil, just a chat between interested parties about a decision overwhelmed by the tragedy.

And later, with camera, interviewing supporters, the Scot I singled out in the Cardiff street said simply to me, 'I'd rather be out of the World Cup and have big Jock back'. It was a perfect summary of how the fans felt about the tragedy.

His collapse at pitch-side has been well documented. His body could not cope with the strain and his altercation with intruding photographers near the end of the game had not helped. Having travelled the world with him I found it difficult to grasp his sudden demise. But through the years I have kept seeing the figure of Davie Cooper linked to that night. Because his two goals that I have recorded here encapsulated the Stein era as national manager. There was the Rangers player's blazing sunshine goal at Hampden that Stein as new manager witnessed and himself likened to the unique personal qualities Cooper possessed. The goal shone with luminous optimism for a new managerial epoch. It was that which took him to the penalty goal in Wales with all its ramifications. That feeling lasted for me all the way through the years to the grim reality of Cardiff which reminded us all of what we were really like as a footballing nation. For any progress in world football would rarely detach us from the looming potential of the pain that too often accompanied it.

49

Heartache

Dundee v Hearts
2–0
Scottish League
3 May 1986
Goal: Albert Kidd

TWO MEN OCCASIONALLY come out of the mists of time leering at me when I think of the day Albert Kidd turned the world upside down for many. They were from opposite sides of the country and as personalities were as different as night is from day.

Inevitably their faces loom up when I think of Kidd and his goals, because of how in different ways they made their mark on me that still rankles. It was all about how they felt I coped when I was sitting on a Dens Park commentary platform that day, having to describe one game whilst listening to reports from another match in Paisley, the news of which would reach Hearts fans in the city of Dundee eventually like being hit by a cyclone.

In the west was a political figure who clearly was a devoted supporter of Celtic and never let an opportunity pass to remind me of such. He was the ex-Lord Provost of Glasgow Michael Kelly, socialist and devout viewer of my programme *Sportscene*, as he could quote me frequently in conversations I would have with him from time to time. He was one of the many in public life who wanted to make it known to me that whatever they were identified for in other areas, they were also football fanatics. And then in the east there was Wallace Mercer, a polar opposite, businessman, whose free-marketeering spirit had motivated him, early on in his incursion into football, to attempt a merger of the two Edinburgh clubs, that was to collapse like the old Tay Bridge in face of a storm of unified local opposition. Kelly was an ascetic, lean figure compared to the Falstaffian Mercer who was extremely popular with the press because of his irrepressible cheeriness and his hospitable arm which always seemed to be within reach of the nearest drinks cabinet. I had encountered Kelly on several footballing occasions with our conversations extremely polite but formal, as if he were keeping his distance from someone he didn't entirely trust. Mercer, on the other hand, could be all over me, although unfailingly and smilingly reminding me of 'my friends in Glasgow', meaning of course the Old Firm with whom he thought I had an unnatural relationship that did Hearts no good. And although I assumed I was dealing with a big fat Tory who liked to give the impression he was glib enough as a salesman to export Portobello sand to Dubai, I enjoyed the blethers and also listening to him expounding on his ambitions for Hearts as they drove on that season with increasing buoyancy, to rid themselves of that 'always the bridesmaid, never the bride' label. He had, though, at the behest of the ex-Hearts player Donald Ford, parted with about £350,000 of his own money to save the club from possible liquidation. Opposites though they were, these two men were almost unified in dissatisfaction as to what I said on a television platform the day Albert Kidd became a legendary executioner.

Although as I sat there just before kick-off on that Saturday neither of the two of them were anywhere near my thoughts. All I was thinking about was the tricky situation I faced in having to keep alert to communications I was assured I would receive from my television director about Love Street, where Celtic were playing St Mirren and whose result could affect what was happening in Dundee. Although, in truth, that seemed highly unlikely at that stage. For Hearts led the division by two points on that final day of the season and only required a draw to clinch the league title at Dens. Even if the Edinburgh side lost, Celtic would still need to beat St Mirren by a considerable margin to pip Hearts. That stacked the odds hugely in favour of the Edinburgh club. Besides, after a shaky start to that season they had gone on a 31-game unbeaten run. So I cannot recall anybody in the media who thought other than that Hearts would win the league title that afternoon. The BBC had no alternative but to have their main cameras at Dens Park for the conclusion.

Dundee though, from the outset, never looked overawed or intimidated in any way by having their stadium packed with maroon and sounding like the Gorgie Road. Their play was exact, firm, organised and in the speed and thrust they showed from time to time looked capable of at least standing up to Hearts uncowed. As for the visitors there is little doubt I admit that I was influenced by their being so close to the title that I made little of the fact that a key player Craig Levein would be missing in central defence. On reflection that had been a severe blow to them. Indeed, I expected an early goal from Hearts with the likes of the two Johns, Robertson and Colquhoun in voracious mood up front. I think it took me about 20 minutes to realise that this was not going to adhere to the kind of presumptive script that I had visualised in my mind. Visualising games beforehand was an instinctive if delusional habit for me.

My director Bill Malcolm was to inform me of any goals 'down by' as we almost flippantly described the other game. I paid little attention to early interruptions in my ear. And then about 11 minutes from half-time with the game at Dens in a state of no-scoring neutrality and the home side giving increasing signs that the title favourites were going to have to work slavishly for their reward, came the words which drew my considerable attention. Bill spoke softly in my ear, 'Celtic are three up now.'

I slammed on the brakes. Immediately. By that I mean I knew now I was about to negotiate a minefield. Yes, if it stayed as it was, a no-scoring draw, then Hearts would still take the title but with an entire half a game yet to play. And having seen the ability of Dundee to break through the Hearts defence from time to time I realised that I was describing men who were now negotiating a veritable precipice and could sense the dense Hearts support realised that well enough now.

The whole tempo of my commentary changed into one of extreme caution. Then came an injury which might now be seen as one of the most historic breakdowns in our game's history. Dundee's Tosh McKinlay picked up a knock and had to be substituted from the bench by one Albert Kidd who, dark, swarthy and broad-shouldered looked sort of mid-European to me as he ran on energetically 16 minutes into the second half. I knew nothing then about him being a devoted Celtic fan. But Dundee improved. The Hearts goalkeeper Henry Smith had to make one of the saves of the season when he was at full stretch to turn a Harvey shot round the post as the game went into the last quarter. Then Bill's voice interceded again, in an early part of the second half, sounding this time almost apocalyptic, 'Celtic are five up now.'

I repeated that into commentary like I was pronouncing an imminent death sentence even though Hearts were still plugging on. The effect on me was that when the first goal did come I was not shocked. It now almost seemed inevitable. There were seven minutes left when Albert Kidd took a headed pass that came to him at waist level and hooked the ball into the net, with a petrified forest of Edinburgh humanity silent and still behind that goal. The second goal, four minutes later, which was like severing the head of an already deceased victim, Messi would have been proud of. Moving from midfield with the ball firmly under his control Kidd played the neatest of one-twos with a colleague before blasting the ball behind Smith. 2–0. That goal was like a stake driven through the heart and is riveted in the mind. Celtic had won the title in their tumultuous 5–0 victory in Paisley. Adulation for Kidd would follow in the days, weeks, months and years ahead from Celtic and Hibernian sympathisers.

We were left viewing emotional debris at Dens in the aftermath as Celtic had won the title by a superior goal difference of +29 to Hearts' 26. Three goals in it, so the scenes of sorrow on the terracing were so vivid that our *Sportscene* team were unanimous in agreeing that we had to show them to the public in our programme later that night. We revealed a community which had waited 16 years for this ultimate prize and it had been snatched from them inside a final seven minutes. A community which rarely touched these heights. Men, women and kids around us were reacting like they had been evicted and left homeless by that cruel landlord in the west. To me it seemed understandable given how close they had been to the promised land. To others it obviously looked mawkish, like I was treating the scenes a bit like the sentimental coverage of the death of Bambi's mother in the Disney film. One such was the ex-Lord Provost of Glasgow Michael Kelly.

The following week he went on a BBC programme and openly attacked me. Since he was fully aware I was not there to rebuff his attack, he waded in. He accused me of departing from the norms of journalistic objectivity for having shown the scenes of distress at Dens and making it clear at the same time how much I sympathised with their distress. Of course, I had been criticised before for comments I had made on several issues, but this was like he had seized on a moment to disclose an unacceptable partiality.

It is true many in the media like myself had been caught up in the swell of Mercer's ebullient promotion of a club and the distinct possibility of Hearts taking the title. We were welcoming something completely new in our game. We had done the same with Fergie and McLean as Aberdeen and Dundee United had dragged us away from the sometimes pedestrian norms of coverage of the Old Firm. This was all so refreshing and clearly we showed appreciation of that in our coverage. Of course, that would suggest partiality to some. But football takes care of itself largely and Celtic did deserve to win the title on footballing merit. Hearts were not good enough at the end of the day.

And there was no solace for me from Mercer who in the first phone-call we had days after the event remarked about how much he had felt I had enjoyed describing the Kidd goals that would please, 'your friends', as he continued to put it! Not bitterly, almost whimsically, like I was a hopeless victim of Glaswegian indoctrination. In that cleft stick of criticism from either side of the country I felt hapless. Then came some sustenance. I read what Albert Kidd himself had told the BBC years later, as quoted on their website by broadcaster David Currie. The scorer had told them this, 'We met the Hearts players in the players' lounge after the match and we really felt for them. It was so sad.' Patronising? Who is ever going to tell of a day which saw such a spectacular clash of emotions?

50

The Crumb of Comfort

Scotland v West Germany
1–2
World Cup Mexico
8 June 1986
Goal: Gordon Strachan

OF ALL THE goal celebrations that have played merrily with the memory through the years, the Gordon Strachan one in the damnable heat of Querétaro in Mexico in 1986 stands out as like somebody who didn't quite know how to register triumph. For some reason he thought he could jump over the advertising hoarding just behind where he had scored the opening goal of the game against West Germany and thought better of it as he looked like he would disembowel himself, stuck as he momentarily became like a hare in a trap, before thinking better of it and freeing himself. Of course he had taken the Germans and, frankly, ourselves, by surprise by penetrating their defence and hitting the net, given the depression we were all suffering after our first game defeat at the hands of Denmark 1–0. Accustomed as we now were to World Cup crises any kind of goal celebration was a sight for sore eyes.

After all we had now taken the lead against the nation which had previously reached the final of the same competition in Spain in 1982. But it gained more significance to me after the tournament ended, standing out, as it did, like the only proof that existed that we had actually been at the World Cup at all. It revived memories of how I was witness to how two different generations of Scottish football were deeply affected by the outcome of that particular game in the steaming hot atmosphere of the city of Querétaro which stood 6,000 feet above sea-level and where frying eggs on the pavements must have been a regular practice there. I think of two men in particular. I think of a young man for whom an unexpected door was opened that day and through which he passed with relish. And I still see the older generation represented by a man for whom that day was protracted torture and almost distorted his legacy as a distinguished Scotland player.

Now when I had arrived in Mexico in the first week I felt almost like I had been cuckolded. My commentary partner in Spain in the previous World Cup had been Billy McNeill whom I had also used for domestic games. We had lost contact with each other when he surprisingly left Celtic for Manchester City in 1983 and started to work occasionally for ITV for whom he was signed up for Mexico. So I appeared on the platform alone to cover Scotland's first game against Denmark. Now, as they say, it's an ill wind that blows no one any good. For there was an unfortunate incident that occurred in that game that was to solve my problem.

Since the draw had been made for the tournament I had tried hard to visualise the sort of opposition the Danes would mount. You play games over in your mind before these big events, but with this opposition I could not summon up any particular style they would inhabit. But I knew they would be technically sound and organised and would possess a Scandinavian purist regard for the laws of the game. I was only right on these first two counts. They were surprisingly adept at the cynical foul that fell just short of a red. They had taken the lead in the 57th minute when Elkjær scored the only goal of the game. You could tell the Scottish players were infuriated at falling behind a team to which they were in no way inferior. They were roused as a result. Roy Aitken thought he had scored an equaliser, shortly after, but the flag had gone up against Charlie Nicholas, who had certainly been looking spritely.

So we now come to what was to solve my commentating problem. Charlie, now closely marked, with ten minutes left, found a gap in which with his speed meant only one defender and the goalkeeper were in front of him. Clenching the mike I would have put money on him to score. Except a defender called Berggreen had other ideas. These were the words Charlie himself spoke to me afterwards. 'I knew I would get the ball to my left foot when I passed him, because although I was predominately right-footed, I always finished better with my left. Suddenly something from the back hit me. I hit the ground. It was brutal. He raked his foot down my leg. It tore my ankle ligaments.'

It was nothing other than an assault that finished Charlie's World Cup, there and then, but astonishingly Berggreen was only yellow-carded. Charlie summed it up perfectly, 'He did it for the team. He took a risk and got away with it.'

Alex Ferguson and his entire coaching staff and players were dismayed that they had lost a game against an average side and at the same time would badly miss an irrepressible striker. They were in no mood to be dealing with anything other than how to reassert themselves after another South American World Cup flop. The manager gave me an interview that was a mix of anguish and determination to put things right against West Germany. Under these circumstances I deferred from mentioning something that had passed through my mind the following day. I waited a couple of days more and then went to see him with the simple request, 'Now that Charlie is out of the reckoning, would you release him to help me in commentary?' I hadn't yet asked the player, nor had I any inkling of how he would cope in a broadcasting situation he had never experienced before. But when it was put to him by the manager Charlie contacted me and agreed to help me out. In fact he looked quite chirpy about it. With that in mind I prepared myself for Querétaro.

The first thing that hit you was the sapping heat. I could not fathom how a proper game of football could be played under these circumstances. So, it was the climate I was first of all concerned with, not predominantly the Germans who could only scramble an equaliser against the Uruguyans with only six minutes remaining in their opening game for the one-all draw. Yes, they had greatly experienced players who had reached the final in Spain and lost to Italy. The irreplaceable Lothar Matthäus still led them and Littbarski, Allofs and Völler all carried threats. And as such I regretted we would not have Alex McLeish in central defence because a sip of the local water had landed him with Montezuma's Revenge and in such a peely-wally condition he ruled himself out, much to the chagrin of Ferguson.

Then about a couple of hours before kick-off Charlie and I became subjects of a contractual dispute. Conversing with Charlie about what our mode of approach should be, since this was all entirely new to him, we were interrupted by a BBC producer who informed us that we would be introducing the programme for the whole of the UK, not just for Scotland, before handing back to network for their own English commentary. We had been promoted. Chuffed as we were, we talked more eagerly about what we would say to the British audience about Scotland's chances. However, about an hour later the same man came back to inform me that Jimmy Hill's agent had insisted that his client had a contract to introduce World Cup programmes and had protested about this idea which had come from *Grandstand* editor John Phillips, a Scot himself. Hill we could see skulking in the shadow of the stand nearby us as we waited for a decision. It came about an hour before kick-off when I was informed that the original plan was confirmed and almost with a sense of triumph Charlie and I moved up to our platform ready to meet our fate. I did introduce the programme and found to my great relief that Charlie was to the manor born, relaxed and chirpy in his chat with me. Kick-off couldn't come quicker after that.

Thirty-thousand watched the steaming efforts of two teams for whom I had the utmost admiration playing in these conditions. I was particularly concerned about the Scottish captain, 33-year-old Graeme Souness. From the outset he looked incapable of coping with the conditions. I refrained from mentioning this to my new partner for some time and let loose with enthusiasm when Scotland opened the scoring in 18 minutes with a brilliant goal. A superb pass from Roy Aitken found Gordon Strachan pouncing on it and from a tight angle swept the ball across Schumacher's body into the net. I enjoyed that moment especially when Strachan simulated a celebration by suggesting he was about to leap over the hoarding. He toyed with the idea to allow us to imagine what it would be like, risking his prostrate if he spliced himself. And, as for the goal, yes, I could hear the encouragement in Charlie's voice about it but with an element of surprise in his voice, given how the Germans had been superior thus far.

They continued to be. It was no surprise when Rudi Völler converted a simple chance in front of goal for the equaliser and under intense pressure we succumbed to Klaus Allofs who scored the winner only five minutes into the second half for an eventual 2–1 win, which could have been worse but for the sterling performance of Jim Leighton in Scotland's goal. I sensed that even with only one goal of a difference with much of the second half remaining, it was time for a gentle inquest. Who were playing their parts and who weren't? Of course the player I had mostly in mind was Graeme Souness, who looked to me simply a fringe player, lacking the pace or the drive and momentum we had first seen as a key feature of Scotland's revival in Mendoza in 1978. Certainly the conditions were affecting him. But he also had much on his mind as the new player/manager of Rangers, of which he was never slow to remind us of out there in Mexico. Was this all too much for him? This is where I had a problem with Charlie. Although he was now a non-playing member of the squad he would still have to go back into the camp mix with his colleagues and face up to Souness with Uruguay still to be faced. But it was unavoidable, or else my role as paid inquisitor would be suspect. So out it eventually came.

'Charlie, is it conceivable that Fergie will drop Graeme for the last game? He just doesn't look fit.'

Without hesitation he replied, 'Graeme is a great player. How do you drop great players?'

As soon as he gave me his answer I knew he was set for a future in television punditry, given how he directly evaded a clear-cut answer but highlighted an understanding of Alex Ferguson's dilemma and the complexity of football management.

We all know Souness was dropped for the last game against Uruguay, a decision that was far from unanimous among the coaching group. Thus, I had witnessed the last time he had worn a Scotland jersey before heading back to revolutionise Rangers and rock Scottish football with the likes of the signing of Mo Johnston, former Celtic player. And I had baptised Charlie Nicholas in the ways of topflight broadcasting and was not surprised to see his regular spritely performances on the Sky football panel years later. So I'm glad Strachan flirted with that pesky hoarding as a colourful reminder not only of the solitary goal we scored in Mexico, but of two men for whom a new destiny beckoned.

51

The English Accent

Aberdeen v Rangers
1–1
League Championship
2 May 1987
Goal: Terry Butcher

FOR ME THERE were two Pittodries. There was the one when Fergie was there. And there was the one when he wasn't. And on that May day when a unique goal was scored it was clear from looking around the stadium just before kick-off that the man who had stamped the name irrevocably on the European map had flown the coop. For how would Fergie, who had turned the stadium into a citadel by a combination of management skills and sheer bravado, have allowed the capitulation of the Aberdeen fans in the face of the invasion from the south? For the Rangers supporters had seized Pittodrie and created Govan-by-the-sea now. The east terracing which normally provided the stadium with its sterling Red Army credentials was now a sea of red, white and blue, as was the beach-end. And those who also came ticketless just to listen, massively outnumbered the seagulls who so often croaked accompaniments to my commentaries there.

Under Fergie that would never have occurred. Somehow or other he would have manipulated events to his advantage regardless of the circumstances which governed the game. Whatever qualities the then Aberdeen manager Ian Porterfield possessed he had none of the tempestuous brio of his predecessor. Fergie, whose relationship with Ibrox was like that of a jilted lover, had utterly exorcised the inferiority complex that had customarily affected Aberdeen in this fixture. Casting my eye around the ground just before kick-off it seemed like Pittodrie had forsaken his legacy. Admittedly, the game meant much more to Ibrox. Rangers were on the verge of winning the Scottish League for the first time in nine years, an incentive for them which they clearly believed would make life worth living again. Optimism bred that huge travelling support because a draw would suffice.

However, contrast the potential tumult of that day to a scene within Ibrox just over a year earlier. David Holmes had been made a director representing the business interests of the tax-exile Lawrence Marlborough. He was a Falkirk man with strong Bairns sympathies. He was so ambitious though for Rangers, whom many, at that time, considered to be no more than a cob-webbed institution in a cul-de-sac, that he got up some journalists noses, one of whom described him as, 'The Joiner from Falkirk who would be the Carpenter from Nazareth.' One day at Ibrox before a match against Hibernian he took part in a pre-match ritual. It was a sweep among the directors, for a fiver each, to see who could guess the size of the crowd that day. He duly wrote down 40,000. It was mocked by those present. In fact the chairman John Paton actually won it with a figure of 13,300, only a few hundred short of the actual figure. Holmes, who could scarcely believe the acceptance of the cosy corner-shop mentality of a club with such massive potential, immediately embarked on a course of action which led to him speedily becoming chief executive and the removal of Jock Wallace the manager.

Now flash forward to the 35th minute of that May day at Pittodrie in 1987. Much has happened since guessing attendances was a favourite diversion in the Ibrox boardroom. Now it was full every week. And we are at a moment in the game when I sense the entire BBC outside broadcast unit is instantly gripped by a feeling that is simply one of sheer incredulity – the jaw-dropping kind. On my earphones I can hear it in the astonished voice of the director Bill Malcolm below me in the van. I can see it in the puzzled look of the technicians beside me on the commentary platform. For how could Rangers player/manager Graeme Souness who had already been booked for a wild tackle, enact a challenge on an opposing player with the subtlety of a combine-harvester, leading with absolute certainty to a red-card, and elimination, with the game goalless and 55 minutes remaining? It was so obvious you had to think he had told his charges, 'I'm going to be sent off and leave you ten to get on with it. It will be the making of you!' Of course, that is a fantasy. But fantasy is as good a route to follow as any to comprehend how a man hungry for personal success, could risk self-harming in such a gratuitous manner. What accompanied that incident though, like in the number of times he offered opportunities for his many detractors outside Ibrox to point to self-evident arrogance, was the sanguine nature he seemed to cope with uproar.

He was sent off after only 34 minutes of his player-manager debut with Rangers at Easter Road, for a tackle on the Hibs player, George McCluskey, that would have been fit for a brawl in a saloon in Tombstone, and after which 21 players were booked. It was as if he had envisaged a headline start of any kind that would waken people to a new dynamic at Ibrox and that he could ride out any adverse publicity which he duly did, despite having given any critics licence to go after him like he was as useful to Scottish society as Asian flu. For instance, his clash with a tea-lady at Muirton Park, Perth, after a game with St Johnstone easily fell into his pursuers' laps who could not fail to portray it as the suffragette standing up to the robber-baron. Add on his recurring jousts with the SFA and the SFL and failing to notice that there were other ears present when he called referee Davy Syme 'a big poof' he nevertheless seemed able to allow controversies to wash over him like they were simply part of a mission that inevitably had to have an ugly side to it. For although it is clear that even some of his strongest supporters did not want such unappealing headlines in newspapers, they would inevitably compare it to Rangers' state of affairs before he arrived. The club had been supine, impotent and feeding off an increasingly distant historical record that was becoming less relevant in the passing of years. What would indiscretions matter if he were to bring success? Rangers now had a big name and a controversialist in power as compared to the eventide-home culture of the previous Ibrox board. That was part of his insurance policy, as well as that very obvious factor, achieving success.

That is why, before they had set off for Aberdeen to try to claim the Championship – the prize they wanted most – the winning of the Scottish League Cup against Celtic, 2–1, after extra-time on 26 October of that season was so crucial. Although not a single Old Firm game has ever encouraged the belief in the brotherhood of man, this was one of the nastiest Old Firm games I ever covered. What was plainly obvious from the outset was that even though an injury had kept him out of that final his reputation as a manager and Rangers' massive spending was on the line so soon after his installation. That mood permeated the entire contest. The whole project could have blown up in the club's face there and then. The sending off of Mo Johnston and his demonstrative crossing of himself as he left the field, and for which his own club fined him, was manna from heaven for the militants on both sides, with the referee Davy Syme coming under special criticism from Celtic manager David Hay who vehemently disagreed with his awarding a penalty to Rangers, from which Davie Cooper scored the winning goal. It was a game for post-match vituperation of the classic Old Firm kind. But crucially for Rangers, Souness had presented the famished support with a trophy. So he didn't operate by the book? What did that matter? And on top of that his gamble in bringing an English accent into the dressing room had paid off in quick time.

Chris Woods, his goalkeeper acquired from the south, had been an England international as had Graham Roberts, the robust midfielder, he was to bring in later that year. But above all he had the iconic figure of Terry Butcher as his natural leader. He wasn't your average English import. He had been that country's Player of the Year in 1985 and whilst his playing abilities could never be in doubt I did wonder at the time how a quintessential Englishman would cope with the unique culture of hostility and all those exotic songs, the choruses of which only had meaning to those brought up among the lyrics of sheer hatred. Did he really know what he was letting himself in for? Well, this is how he put it to me himself some years after he had left Scotland.

'I got caught in the atmosphere far too much. My wife said I went from one extreme to the other, from being a naïve Englishman not knowing anything about it to becoming someone sucked into the hatreds too much. I ended up with an immense hatred for Celtic, not on religious grounds but just as our greatest rivals. And in general we bonded well in working up the belief that everybody was against us, so to hell with them, just beat them!'

These leadership qualities were now to be put to the test at Pittodrie with his manager now off the field. The game itself was tight, nervy. You could not tell if the untidy scrap would yield anything of class, given the quality of defending on both sides. On the one hand, Willie Miller at the back for Aberdeen once again conveyed the impression to me that he hardly ever broke sweat, but constantly aided by his unique sense of timing he could look unpassable. On the other side you could clearly witness the height and presence of Butcher and his constant yelling and bawling was getting the upmost out of the depleted ranks.

Now the Rangers goal that effectively won them the title was special. Not in a technical sense. Five minutes from half-time a free kick invitingly floated into that Aberdeen penalty area from the talented left foot of Davie Cooper, meeting the rising head of an unmarked centre-half, Butcher, who powered it into the net. I had seen this performed in many a game by others. It was straight out of the textbook. It was who scored it that made it so different. As the ball hit the net Butcher celebrated like he was to the parish born. A wildly celebrating former English captain effectively winning Rangers the league title was as rare a spectacle in Scottish football as the sighting of polar bear on Arran. Now our cameras immediately sought in vain to see if they could portray Souness's reaction to that spectacle and for me to summon up some kind of comment about the indiscretion that had separated him from that historic moment. But he was nowhere to be seen. Nor did I ever discover where he was when the historic goal that won them the title was scored. It seemed to me a bit like a father choosing the hospital café for a cuppa rather than witnessing the delivery of a firstborn.

Aberdeen's big defender Irvine equalised five minutes later to make it 1–1 but thereafter Aberdeen were simply not good enough to break down a Rangers side which while not playing with any great finesse, held their ground. Souness, wherever, probably heard before the players he had deserted on the field, that Falkirk had also beaten Celtic that same afternoon to underscore Rangers' triumph. And it was indeed a triumph even if you reduced it to a single game of ten against 11. But, of course, it was more than that. Souness's indiscretion which could have cost the club mightily could not possibly mar a day which many of the club's supporters were beginning to feel would never be reached again.

I did not speak to him that day. But I couldn't fail to mention in my eventual summation of the game, the interview he had given me on the other side of the world in Santa Fe just before moving with the rest of the Scotland squad to the World Cup finals in Mexico and just after his appointment to Ibrox. Without blinking he had stated to me, 'And I don't care if Celtic beat us four times in the league as long as we win the Championship. We have to get rid of the traditional mind-set. People will have to change.'

Despite his bewildering personal failing that day at Pittodrie he could now claim he had the mass conversion powers of a Billy Graham.

52

The Pyrrhic Victory

Celtic v Rangers
1–0
Scottish Cup Final
20 May 1989
Goal: Joe Miller

THE 13TH OLD Firm final was the most cosmopolitan of them all. By kick-off, with a roasting sun in ascendancy, so were the English players in the Rangers side. There were six of them. Chris Woods, Gary Stevens, Terry Butcher, Mel Sterland, Mark Walters and Kevin Drinkell. This was the Souness revolution in its full flowering. Celtic had three Irish, Pat Bonner, Chris Morris and Mick McCarthy, plus Englishman Anton Rogan. I immediately pointed to the presence of ten non-Scots on the field. However, ideally there ought to have been seven Anglos in blue. But Ray Wilkins was injured and Rangers badly missed him in an undistinguished midfield battle. And it was hot. Perhaps the steamiest of all the finals I ever commentated on. And of course I am not referring to the normal sectarian analogy we usually refer to which produces its own heat and clamminess, but that physical dehydration could eventually be a factor for players on that sun-bleached pitch.

It would have taken more than a sudden cold front, though, sweeping down from the Arctic circle to moderate the surrounds of Ibrox Park. Rangers were on fire, as we would say. They were coming straight from having engulfed Pittodrie, winning the title, and it seemed that the policy that their player/manager Graeme Souness had adopted, of Anglicising his side in part, had paid off handsomely now that they held both the

Championship and the League Cup. My preview cup final interview with the player/manager at Ibrox, the day before a game which could give him the treble in his first season in Scottish football, was like dealing with a purring cat which had just downed its cream. No showboating. No particular claims. But a self-evident satisfaction that fell well short of blatant self-confidence. And Souness was especially keen to pay tributes to his players at the same time, although failing to confirm if he would select himself for the final or not. It was like listening to an inoffensive, bland, peroration of a man quietly accepting the fact his side were favourites to lift the treble.

At Celtic Park in the equivalent interview with Billy McNeill, despite the fact that the club had had a poor season, as reflected in Rangers' success, Billy McNeill the manager seemed in no way cowed. Several factors were in play with him. Firstly, we had built up a good relationship through our broadcasting partnerships especially in the World Cup. We never failed to recount some of the incidents that we had experienced particularly with 007 in Spain. It always elevated our chats above the ordinary. Secondly, he had unprecedented experience of Old Firm matches and knew how in that tradition many of us in the media had fallen into the trap of using current form to make predictions and had come unstuck. Over and above that he was well-inured to this unique pressure having come through different stages of the Celtic experience, from the uncertain days of the McGrory era, through to lifting the European Cup in Lisbon under Stein. He would carry that positively into the dressing room with him on the day. What he warned me in advance though, is that he would not talk about Mo Johnston, a player who would not be taking part in the final but was in the news in a big way.

Mo was the talk of the steamie in fact. His name was on the lips of every Celtic fan. A press conference had been arranged only a week prior to the final where the former striker had been displayed in a green and white jersey, pen in hand, not only symbolising his love of a club he had left for Nantes in France in 1987, after scoring 52 goals in 100 appearances for Celtic but lending the strong impression of contractual commitment as well. But McNeill deliberately declared confidence in the current strike force that would be at Hampden and mentioned Joe Miller particularly by name who would be given the outright striker's role in the absence of the injured Andy Walker. Although at the time I thought that was simply understandable window-dressing, set against the Johnston fever running through the ranks of supporters. Of course, admittedly I had no knowledge of what was happening inside Celtic Park about this issue, except that we all knew that the manager's former dealings with the chairman Desmond White had resulted in him leaving for Manchester City in 1983. Surely the current board would have learned lessons from that period?

Like others, I expected Rangers, as strong favourites, to benefit from having put the league title behind them and simply pick up from the momentum the ten men had shown at Pittodrie. But it never appeared. Complacency? Or was it the fact that a hardworking Celtic side, again inspired by the commitment of Roy Aitken in midfield, constantly reminded Rangers that in this fixture in particular walkovers were rarities? Because after half an hour of this final, if you had no knowledge of the previous weeks' form you could not really tell who were the favourites to win.

Then came the goal. Souness had bought quality, particularly in defence where Butcher reigned supreme. Around him were also English internationals who responded well to the former England captain. Their competence had never been in question. Until that moment. A ball was played through the middle into Rangers' penalty area but looked well within the capacity of the Rangers defence to deal with. Except that Gary Stevens, in a casual manner attempted a pass-back to his keeper Chris Woods. It was badly misjudged and was seized upon by Joe Miller who promptly stroked it into the back of the net. This gift was presented to Celtic with only four minutes left to play in the first half. There was much of the game to come and the expectancy that Rangers' current form would produce a positive response in the time available dominated the proceedings from then on.

Now I admit that in my commentary style, I tended to build up the nature of the divide between two teams with the emphasis on the side behind trying to catch up. I continued to pose questions about Rangers' ability to equalise and perhaps less about Celtic's capability to hold them at bay. That pattern would certainly have sounded partial to certain ears. But something certainly did pass me by that had a huge bearing on the outcome. The Celtic goal had stemmed from an incident on their right touchline. In a challenge with a Rangers player we could see in the aftermath of the game that the ball had in all probability come off Aitken last before going out of play. But he had seized the ball and taken a quick throw-in which would lead eventually to the move upfield and the only goal of the game. Graeme Souness made much of that incident after the match without eliciting much sympathy from neutrals who were more fascinated by his side's inability to find an equaliser.

That win engineered by McNeill against the favourites, would not cement his relationship with the club he loved above all and to us outsiders caused wonderment that he could be treated the way he had been especially in the Mo Johnston affair. Clearly, he wanted the striker back. But when he was on holiday in Florida Celtic's board severed all connections with the Mo promoters. Having just won the Scottish Cup against the favourites and traditional rivals they were in a strong position to do so. That's when the significant men who backed Rangers perked up their ears and began to think the previously unthinkable. When Jack Irvine editor of *The Sun* in Scotland heard the strength of the rumour of Rangers' possible interest he sent the assistant sports editor Iain Scott out to Italy to the Ibrox summer training camp in the truly beautiful setting of Barga in the Tuscan hills to scavenge for any news on that possibility. He returned only with hints about the possibility of such a transaction. However, in Scott's own words he told his editor, 'I think he's signed him.' On that basis alone *The Sun* scrapped what was being prepared and instead devoted a whole 16 pages to a definite transfer of Johnston to Rangers – again in Scott's own words – 'We took an almighty gamble!' It paid off handsomely. As did Souness's.

53

Topsy Turvy

Rangers v Celtic
1–0
Scottish Championship
4 November 1989
Goal: Mo Johnston

THAT EXCELLENT JOURNALIST Neil Cameron wrote this in the *Glasgow Evening Times* of the game above. 'Go watch the footage now. There is nobody with their arms folded doing the old Presbyterian thing of doing their best not to enjoy something. Instead, everyone seems to be having a good time, utterly uncaring of what school the match-winner had gone to.' He was writing about a very special goal indeed that won a game with only two minutes left on the clock. But I will come to that later.

I received a telephone call on the morning of 4 October 1989 from my son. He told me that there was a virulent rumour doing the rounds in his work that very morning that Mo Johnston had signed, or was about to, for Rangers after *The Sun* had carried that huge story about an imminent transfer which had been relegated by many of us to fantasy. So the men in the work had got together and asked my son if he would inquire of the man who was supposed to know everything that was going on in Scottish football, if there was any credibility to those whispers. Of course, that man was me. But I remember well my quote to him, word for word. It was, 'Tell them there is more chance of the Pope signing for Rangers than Mo Johnston!' So the man who was supposed to know everything about what was going on in our game told them to forget it. Nonsense. About half an hour later I received a call from the BBC telling me that a press conference had been called at Ibrox and although they had no knowledge of its contents, it sounded important enough, and I should get there post-haste. So the man who was supposed to know about everything that was going on in the game, left for the stadium slightly weak at the knees. 'Surely not?' was the recurring thought of my own credibility being at stake among workers in an office. Indeed, when I arrived at Ibrox there was a small crowd outside, one of whom shouted out to me. 'Is it true, Archie?' The man who was supposed to know everything about Scottish football ignored that and climbed the marble staircase. I asked a photographer coming down the stairs, 'Is he there?' He nodded assent and I started thinking of excuses for having been an outright sceptic of what now appeared to have been one of the most sensational manoeuvres in Scottish football history.

The Rangers blazer they had put on Mo for the occasion did not fit. It made him look like he had picked the wrong one in the rush out of school. And you could tell *The Sun* journalists by their chests bursting proudly out of their jackets having scooped all of us! Mo stared out into space scarcely believing it himself and barely opened his mouth before being swept away by a fatherly Souness. I suppose that being aware of Mo's colourful social life in which he knew more about the stations around Europe than the Stations of the Cross, that religion and the breaking of this Ibrox tradition, did not seem at that moment in time in the stately boardroom, as if the foundations of football were quaking. Mo, in his outsized blazer, did not carry the bearings of an historic icon. Yes, we were to hear tales of Ibrox season tickets being cancelled and some of his playing colleagues not wishing to be photographed alongside him at any time. Personally, I saw or heard nothing about that and the Ibrox maximum attendances never altered, which was like nothing had changed. After all, their supporters, as did those of their traditional opponents, interpreted this in another way. The Rangers financial advisers had shafted Celtic. It was an acute embarrassment suffered most of all by the man who just before had paraded Mo as a profligate son about to return to the fold, Billy McNeill.

But, yes, at street level this was the stuff to keep the traditionalists plundering it for all their worth, one way or the other. Understandably the Celtic following viewed it as a brazen act of treachery. His identity with the Celtic community could not have been made clearer in the Scottish League Cup final of 26 October 1986 when being sent off he pointedly made the sign of the Cross directed towards the Rangers end. An alien might have made nothing of that, but the rest of the indigenous crowd knew exactly what it meant! But now he seemingly had made an allegiance to the green and white colours seem as durable as an ice cream on a hot summer's day.

And, as we could hardly ignore that fact, we discussed it sometimes, I am sorry to say, like we were assessing the historical relevance of Judas Iscariot, who as far as we know had little knowledge of freedom of contract issues. It was simply the ending of a preposterous tradition that had it persisted would have encircled Rangers in a parochial enclosure of self-destruct, particularly in European football. What was really happening of significance was the entrance of the money men into football to keep company with those who would know how to spend their cash in the game. The Nevada-based Lawrence Marlborough's wealth and delegating the astute David Holmes to directorship of the club to represent his interests undoubtedly strengthened Souness's hand as did the banning of English clubs from European competition in the wake of the Heysel Stadium disaster, thus offering them an avenue into Europe. When David Murray's £6,000,000 acquired Rangers from Marlborough in 1988 at least we had someone on home territory whom we thought might be easily accessible. Six years later Fergus McCann was to enter the scene when in March 1994 with Celtic on the brink of insolvency, he flew from Phoenix, Arizona where he was conducting his highly successful golf-travel company and with only about ten minutes to spare lodged the required amount to save the club from receivership.

I found neither of these men easy to deal with. Murray always seemed to speak over my head to another audience, constantly aware of self-image to the point of self-idolatry. Although you could not but admire how the loss of both legs in a horrendous motor-car accident did not deter him from being a highly successful businessman. McCann was more a football man having served his time as a supporter with Croy Celtic Supporters Club in his early days. But I could feel they both viewed me with suspicion. They really had nothing much to say to me but through professional duty I was propped up in front of them occasionally to go through a rigmarole of formal innocuous questions that was getting us nowhere. The difficulty for me was that I always wanted to direct them towards the football, or put another way, to find out what was going on inside the heads of the respective managers out of public interest. I would have got more out of the Sphinxes.

Certainly McCann was more interesting before he took over Celtic. When he was on the rampage against the existing board then, he and his interviewer Hugh Keevins of Radio Clyde were thrown out of the stadium for what was considered unfair comments and had to finish their chat outside in the radio car. Of course it was the football which would decide their fates regardless of their commitment to either club and their dexterity with money. That is why Mo playing in a blue jersey at Celtic Park on 26 August 1989 created so much interest. Back in his homestead, but in a new uniform, made him a target of constant abuse, but little other than that. He was mocked when he missed two clear chances in that game but the 1–1 draw satisfied all that nobody had caused disgrace of any kind.

It was their next encounter which did affect people on both sides.

I arrived on the television platform of Ibrox on the 4 November 1989 determined not to let Mo steal the show. He was not there to perform tricks for us but to be part of a Rangers team which would be attempting to maintain their splendid recent record against their old foes at the stadium where Celtic had conceded nine goals and four points during the previous season. I found myself trying manfully to make him just a player with a specific number on his jersey, and in a sense, amidst those doubting-Thomases in blue and the outright haters in green in the stands, he was aiding me by simply being almost anonymous in a disappointing game. We certainly noticed him protecting his face when after running to collect a ball for a throw-in near Celtic supporters he had to cover it when half-time pies were aimed at his face. No, it was all about the ending. I think I had been affected by the sheer plod of the game and that I was struggling to sound really involved, when we entered the last five minutes. However, Spielberg would have rejected the ending as too preposterous to put on film and even yet it is scarcely believable.

Two minutes to go Stevens makes a run on the right and his cross is only weakly cleared by the Celtic defender Morris to the feet of Mo on the edge of the box. His shot is not power-driven but angled with a precision which clearly had not been distorted by his change of colours, to pass the outstretched hand of Celtic goalkeeper Pat Bonner into the net. Rangers have won the game and the stadium's reaction is as near to mass astonishment as I can ever recall.

Mo's reaction is like a cradle-born Rangers supporter, running off the pitch to share his emotions with the same crowd who had mocked him previously for his dramatic gesture in a final that seemed to suggest they were a heathen flock. Or, as I watched his delirium, looking like a man released from solitary confinement, having proved the falsity of ridiculous comments about his real commitment. So, the man who was supposed to know everything about Scottish football praised Souness publicly for his audacious coup with, I admit, like him, little immediate concern about how a decent young man could live now hated by an entire community for the rest of his life.

54

A Sending Off

Rangers v Celtic
1–0
Scottish Cup Semi-Final
31 March 1992
Goal: Ally McCoist

ALLY MCCOIST AND Charlie Nicholas wore different colours but many of the goals that came from both of these men were remarkably alike. They were simply twinned in opportunism. The choice of a selection of a single goal out of the many is like a gluttonous kid being allowed the freedom to pillage Rowntree's sweetie factory. But this significant goal comes to mind easily because of who was sitting in the dugout that evening. Walter Smith. He was Ally's fourth Rangers manager and somebody special. The revolving goal of management had made for circumstances that Charlie at Celtic never had to face. He had his own intrinsic problems there. For a striker like Ally though having to face four different managerial attitudes to football, in the one club, put him in a more demanding environment. At times he admitted that when he felt he had fallen out of favour within the dressing room and on the terracings, that it made him a much wiser and tougher individual. Certainly he always wanted to be at Ibrox, and John Greig when he left the club in the autumn of 1983 after the defeat in the Scottish Cup final against Fergie's Aberdeen could at least boast of his ultimately disappointing reign, that he signed from Sunderland a player whose scoring feats were to win him many honours including winning Europe's Golden Boot award twice in 1992 and 1993 as leading goalscorer of all the continent's major leagues.

And yet with my own ears at Love Street, against St Mirren in Greig's final year, when our commentary position was much closer to supporters, I was surprised at the invective he was getting from what I have to say was a fickle Rangers support which that day had made up their minds he was a waste of space, or even worse, in their creative critical ways of pinning blame. Yes, it wasn't his day. A day of missed chances certainly, as I recall. I think though it was a reflection of the malaise that had overtaken Ibrox as a whole with the manager's days numbered. And I certainly recall that period when Ibrox seemed to be in limbo, with the board dithering about whom to turn to next and had even looked northwards to the wee man at Tannadice who ultimately took cold feet at the prospect. But living close to me in Bothwell was the Motherwell manager, a certain Jock Wallace. He was so desperate to return to his first love Rangers that he actually phoned me and was openly blunt on the matter. 'Why don't they effing well come for me?' he asked. Frankly, Wallace was always a pleasant man to deal with, his gruff manner belying a softer inner soul. But he informed me of his eventual appointment to the job in a rather usual way. I answered the phone late one evening and listened to a man singing the 'Sash'. It was Wallace's way of informing me that Ibrox had turned to him, although his use of the party song was simply one of the gauche and deliberately calculated ways he would continue to play to the gallery. At least he was a boost to Ally initially but with new faces applying new thinking to the future of the club he was ousted six years later and in came Souness applying severe strictures to Ally's independently minded way of thinking and embracing Mo Johnston with obvious implications.

But beside Souness there was another face. Walter Smith sat to the side and at the back in one of the first press conferences I attended inside Ibrox, ruminatively, deliberately playing the role of a new assistant who knew his place. But then he was practised at that. I had known him for years shadowing Jim McLean at Tannadice like he had been appointed by Special Branch to keep an eye on royalty. There was no other way he could have served there because any time you entered that domain the little manager engulfed you. He allowed nothing or anybody to pass him and it meant that for years I was only on nodding terms with the man who would arguably become Rangers most renowned manager. But clearly something had been brewing constantly when he was there, for Walter was working with a manager who had one of the keenest football brains I had ever come across, and sometimes you could feel like a novice listening to McLean open your eyes to the complexities of the game with a professionalism that took both of them to a UEFA final. Walter indeed was part of a unit that almost qualified for the European Cup final itself in 1984 when I watched them being virtually assaulted by the Roma players on the field even though they had just knocked United out 3–0 in that semi-final.

So on that 31 March evening, with Souness gone Walter was now a manager in the full and had put his trust in a striker who had had a lean day ten days before when Celtic had beaten Rangers 2–0 at Ibrox for their 11th straight win in a row. I recall Ally having only one shot in that entire game. But he was selected again by a manager who certainly had failed at his first Old Firm test and was now considered an under-dog for this match. A position he had been accustomed to at Tannadice. He was also minus the other half of the striking force, with Hateley out injured. But, of all the time he was in Dundee, I believe he would never be able to recall a game like the one that evening at Hampden in the driving wind and rain. Not because of the elements. For I certainly left the stadium that night utterly bemused by its outcome. It hinged on an incident in the 10th minute of the game when David Roberston of Rangers bodychecked Joe Miller of Celtic in midfield in a manner a Scottish full-back at Murrayfield might have admired. Referee Andrew Waddell sent him off. Now let me admit that as a commentator I hated 11 against 10 men games. It's not what you came prepared to comment on; an equal battle. Yes, of course, it could produce drama, controversy and inspire you to rise to a level well above the normal. But in these circumstances, which I experienced several times through the years, I always felt I was acting under constraint not to show too much sympathy to the handicapped side.

The single goal that meant not just the winning of the game but so much to Rangers' history, came just before half-time. And it was itself a product of the sending off, because it was at a period when Celtic were throwing everything at Rangers' ten men and in the logic of these circumstances lost focus on defending. In a sharp counter-attack Stuart McCall was pivotal in the run forward, the control of the ball and the accuracy of his neat square pass to the on-rushing Ally just outside the box. The conditions were appalling and the greasy pitch was now more amenable to howling mistakes than accuracy. And Ally, remember, was a figure under great pressure because of his dismal form of the previous game at Ibrox where he took a lot of the critical heat for being posted absent when being beaten on home turf. And because of that, as he stroked the ball with the inside of his foot I wondered afterwards how many, even of the diehard supporters thought he would tuck it away successfully. But he did, confidently, although even amidst the wild celebrations you had to wonder how Rangers could hold out for the whole of the second half. It is difficult to understand why Celtic did not score in that period. It was a unique siege for an Old Firm game. And yet when you recorded the missed opportunities you began to actually believe something approaching a miracle was in view. For there were a whole series of missed chances and I recall the outstanding Paul McStay hitting the underside of the bar, but the ball failing to drop over the line. Andy Goram in the Rangers goal was like a magnet to the mostly erratic shooting. Rangers even survived a strong appeal for a penalty when John Collins appeared to have been brought down in the area by John Brown but Andrew Waddell was now in a more charitable mood from a Rangers perspective after the sending off and disallowed it. But the pressure was so intense that assistant manager of Rangers Archie Knox asked a ball-boy at half-time if he was a Rangers fan and gave him a fiver with the following instruction 'If the ball goes out for a Celtic throw-in, just leave it until the Celtic fans throw it back. If the ball goes out for a Rangers throw-in, just leave it full stop.'

We have never discovered how influential the juvenile Mafioso was on that late evening but I believe at one stage I thought I detected the Celtic heads dropping in sheer frustration (waiting for balls to be thrown back?) which accompanied the feeling that the Ibrox side were going to hold out after all. It was a creditable achievement though and Celtic being against ten men for so long they could not really cry 'Injustice' too loudly. So Rangers moved on to the final where Walter lifted his first Scottish Cup in beating Airdrie 2–1. So, of the many Ally goals I could have pinpointed why is that one so prominent in the mind? For several reasons. For it was the first goal Rangers had scored against Celtic in that competition since 1973 and it was like Ally had opened a door to Walter with an invitation to pass through and prove himself at other levels. For the manager was now completely free of the Souness influence, totally independent, winning his first silverware and leading Rangers into a new era, out of the shadow of that former miner from Burnbank who had started the treasure hunt of ten-in-a-row so long ago.

55

Mishap

Brazil v Scotland
2–1
World Cup Opening Ceremony and Match
10 June 1998
Goal: Tom Boyd (OG)

IT FELT LIKE emasculation. It really did. Even to someone like myself who believed he had seen it all and could swallow anything that football could dish up. I watched the ending of that game like I was witnessing a scene devised by a comedy writer who did not realise how an entire nation could not see the funny side of what he had intended. And I felt particularly isolated even amidst so many Scots in the stadium and streets. For in that period I was in exile in the City of Light. And, yes, Paris has enough creature comforts to ease any serious yearnings you might have for the old country. Indeed it's fair to say it can even make you forget where you came from in the first place. But a bizarre goal had made me feel like I was a displaced person.

I had been hired by *Eurosport,* to put my English language voice to commentaries for the UK and wherever I could be understood around the continent. It was a multi-lingual station incorporating a variety of languages and during a few years in and out of that beautiful city I learned to say 'Good morning' at breakfast in the hotel in French, Dutch, Portuguese, German, Swedish, Norwegian and Spanish, to my fellow commentators who like me were still trying to come to terms with this new style of commentating. For until the World Cup finals were based in France in 1998, we commentated from a distance. You would sit in a tiny cubicle, earphones clamped round the head and rivet your attention to the screen of a monitor where tiny figures played out these games.

As you might readily understand it was fraught with potential problems. To perform recorded highlights I would refrain from learning any score before entering the booth, so that I could commentate spontaneously as if it were live. But on one occasion Celtic had been drawn to play Sporting Lisbon in the UEFA cup in season 1993–94 and won the first leg narrowly 1–0. I stayed away from any news of the second leg in Lisbon and went into the Paris booth wound up for a demanding second leg. When I commentated on the tie ending 1–1 on aggregate having talked about Sporting's excellent goal, but noticed their players celebrating as if they had actually won the tie, I knew something was wrong. As the programme came to an end, I actually declared that we were now going into extra-time, although admittedly it was an unusual way to see the home players celebrating extra-time. I was bemused. In fact someone in the editing suite had inadvertently cut-out Lisbon's winning goal to make it 2–1 without informing me. So I promoted an extra-time period to come to a vastly diverse European audience that never actually occurred. This was typical of the crudities of this young station attempting to establish itself throughout the continent as a credible means of presenting European football to a wide audience.

So it was with a sense of enormous relief that we learned that *Eurosport*'s coverage of the 1998 World Cup in France would be from commentating sites in the stadiums themselves. And of course I was excited about performing at the opening ceremony and match at the Stade de France between Brazil and ourselves once again. And this time there would be no allowance for any mishaps like the one above in that tiny booth, as it was estimated this game would have a live television audience of 500 million people in 195 countries, all of which would make working for *Eurosport* out in the open seem like I was joining in the *Hallelujah Chorus*. This would be the fifth time I had had both the privilege and perhaps, dubious pleasure, of venting my thoughts on these games against the South Americans. And of course there were two elements I could never forget. Firstly, the best of our performances. That was in 1966 in the pre-World Cup tournament in England when they came to Hampden and discovered that a spindly-legged individual called Baxter had nothing to learn from them about artistry in a football and was outstanding in the 1–1 draw. Then there was the German World Cup in 1974 and that moment in the no-scoring draw in Frankfurt when in front of an open goal and the ball sweeping toward him on a few yards out Billy Bremner's legs froze and one of our best chances of ever beating a well below par Brazil side vanished. There really was one game when Brazil played the way we anticipated and thrashed us 4–1 and that was in Seville in retribution for the David Narey 'toe-poke'. The 1–0 defeat by them in 1990 which came only nine minutes from the end of the game was utterly featureless. Now they were a side dominated by the presence of one Ronaldo who at the tender age of 20, two years previously, had been named FIFA World Player of the Year. As always I looked forward to watching brilliant football on display whatever the result although inwardly hoping that that brilliant young player would have had a night out on the tiles in Montmartre before the game and would be suffering a migraine at kick-off. I was at the stage when I would accept any circumstances just to get a win over them after having watched so many minutes of subservience.

I certainly had trust in the Scottish manager Craig Brown whom I knew full well did not satisfy every Scottish customer decorating the Champs-Élysées in these preceding days. He was the product of the sudden change of tact of the secretary of the SFA Ernie Walker in 1986 when he surprised us all by appointing Andy Roxburgh, former headmaster of a primary school, as manager of the national side. Brown was a continuation of that species, but with the added dimension for me of having known him since he was a schoolboy and actually, as a student I refereed him once in a schools' cup game when he was a pupil at Hamilton Academy. A committed, hardworking player then, as he continued to be in later life, although having moved to Rangers firstly, despite his father's open criticism of the way they played their game in the days of Struth, it was the start of an honest but undistinguished football career with Dundee and Falkirk. He moved into education and was both teacher and lecturer which was the kind of aspect of his life some of his critics could not square with football expertise and both he and Roxburgh were occasionally dismissed as the 'Largs Mafia' for their coaching courses down by the coast which were deemed merely talking shops of little merit. This absurd sloganising only increased my respect for Brown in particular who engaged in chats with me that were always illuminating, particularly the way he seemed to assess his players individually. They were intimates.

So watching him walk out ahead of a Scots team unselfconsciously and proudly wearing kilts, it was as if to remind the French in the crowd of the historic Auld Alliance between the two countries. They did not look intimidated by the immediate prospect of taking on the tournament's favourite side. Yes, the initiative always seemed with the Brazilians although after a while it was obvious that Brown's strategy of caution and respect was making it awkward for the South Americans. And above all the Scots had steeled themselves particularly for this day as explained by Darren Jackson. 'I wasn't in the slightest bit nervous. I was probably more nervous when I started off playing games for Meadowbank. But there I was standing beside Ronaldo, the most famous player in the world and yet I felt like I was privileged to be there. Not a single nerve did I feel.'

Not that that composure could help prevent the opening basic goal. Four minutes into the game Brazil were awarded a corner-kick. Bebeto swung in what seemed an innocuous cross which César Sampaio, unchallenged, glanced into the net. This was the first time in the 56 goals conceded in 70 games during the Brown reign that Scotland had conceded a goal from a corner-kick. That fact stung throughout the media corps. What compensated in a major way was a delectable moment eight minutes from half-time when the referee turned benevolent towards Scotland. Durie rose to a cross from Burley who knocked the ball to Kevin Gallagher coming across the penalty area. César Sampaio brushed against him. Gallagher fell forward. Penalty. Let me lay against the referee's prompt decision, the words of Gallagher spoken to me some time after the game.

'It was the first time I ever dived in my career,' he told me, then went on to elaborate. 'I remember when we played Sweden in one of the qualifying games. I recall being pushed in the back, but I kept on my feet when I should have gone down. This time I did.'

John Collins took the penalty and although Taffarel guessed right and almost got to it, the ball ended in the net with the Scottish crowd demonstrating to the world how well they could celebrate. But the ending was crippling. The Brazil winning goal is still nightmarish to me and others. Jim Leighton in goal had not been busy after the equaliser and the game looked to be slipping away in neutrality, although with Brazil looking attractive on the ball. To talk to Tom Boyd about that moment that changed everything is like talking to a man who felt fate had played a treacherous trick on him and that there was nothing that he could have done to alter the outcome. Anybody who witnessed it could see he was utterly an innocent party. He described to me painfully what then was to occur.

'Ok, I thought I could get a cut-back from Cafu and keep my eye on Ronaldo. Cafu then doesn't cut it back, but hits it towards goal. Jim, in goal, palms it out and in my effort to get back, the rebound hits me in the chest and I was hoping that Colin Hendry had the pace I'd never thought he had before and would get to the ball. But I knew it was a forlorn hope. It hit the net and I was gutted. And, do you know, years later people still have a wee dig at me about that. But it's never been hostile. It's always been good-natured banter.'

Tom Boyd, a Scot obviously still in harmony with an understanding community who over the World Cup years had learned how to live with disappointment. And I was to discover, in the immediate aftermath, that even amidst some of the most attractive watering-holes you can find anywhere in the world, Paris could be as appealing as a dry bothy in the Outer Hebrides after an outcome like that. The feeling of injustice followed me around the streets of the city like I was being pursued by the hunchback of Notre Dame. And it was in Paris, after the 3–0 debacle against Morocco in St Etienne in our last game that I had to listen to commentators from around Europe in the resplendent *La Coupole* restaurant summarising the finals and talking about Scotland as if our football was simply unfit for this exalted level of the game. And they tore into our World Cup record reaching the conclusion that we were hardly ever likely to qualify out of the group stages – that is in the unlikely event of us ever reaching the finals again. In the middle of this onslaught of criticism, meant particularly for my ears, I found it difficult to find the right words to counter such withering comments that attributed us to permanent mediocrity. As of now, I am still searching for them.

56

Sayonara Spectacle

Celtic v Manchester United
1–0
Champions League Game
21 November 2006
Goal: Shunsuke Nakamura

MANY STRIKES TOOK the breath away as they were intended to do. One still does. Which is why it is here now. When STV after the World Cup in France game invited me back to commentate on their channel it opened up the Champions League to me again and to a moment that got me out of my commentating position like I was a pilot ejecting from his seat in mid-air flight. And for the first time I had to deal with names that simply seemed alien to our traditional way of thinking of Scottish football. For on the team sheet was a Japanese name. Easy enough to pronounce. But how different from Charles Patrick Tully, all those years ago. Now I am old enough to remember when people hated the Japanese. My uncle Andrew fought against them in the jungles of Burma in the 1940s and the tales he told of the way they fought and how they treated prisoners of war gave me nightmares. In the local cinema the *Palaceum* in Shettleston I devoured films like *Objective Burma,* starring inevitably Errol Flynn and which was highly successful in being nominated for three Oscars because in post-Pearl Harbour American society they simply portrayed the Japanese as evil little yellow heathens, largely without question. And as far as I can recollect I don't think I was all that distressed on hearing of the atomic retributions at Hiroshima and Nagasaki. It is difficult to know when that distant country after the war offered itself with an entirely reconstructed identity to myself, who was getting on with life, and interpreting the world increasingly through the eyes of a football lover to the expense of much else.

I certainly never really associated Japan with football. The American occupation had slanted them towards baseball which meant their sporting mentality was attuned more to the New York Giants than say Real Madrid, or so I believed. Of course they were progressing from amateurism to organised professionalism and I can recall hearing of their hosting and winning the 1992 Asian Cup by defeating Saudi Arabia 1–0 in the final. It made as much impact on me as hearing the result of a camel race in Afghanistan. No, there was only one name that awakened me to a wholly changed world where football had sown its seeds in apparently alien ground but the fruits of which were now heading Scotland's way.

He was Shusune Nakamura.

Although I heard Gordon Strachan was signing such a player from the Italian club Reggina, a look at his origins including playing for Yokohama Marinos in the Japanese league suggested something of a gamble, and a desperate one at that since Celtic had started the 2005 season indifferently and looked at times rudderless. And it was one thing to move from a Japanese climate into Italy with less of a dramatic climatic change than coming here, for how would a fine touch player, as we assumed he would be, put up with the 'glaur' of a Scottish winter. I did not cover his opening game against Dundee United. But the reports were good. He was named Man of the Match. Promising certainly, but was it simply over-optimism? By the end of that season though when Celtic had won the Premier League and the Scottish League Cup and Nakamura was now an electric stimulus to Celtic's forward momentum, Gordon Strachan must have felt like he might be able to turn his hand into sorting out the world economy which was just about to head into the Great Recession. And, of course it was in Europe in the next season Nakamura was to cement his relationship with the club forever, during which he forced a commentator and his assistant into one impulsive balletic dance on a television platform one night.

As Nakamura had moved his world, so had I. Full circle almost. From BBC to Clyde to Eurosport and now STV, eerily, in a way, filling the shoes of my old friend but television adversary of the past, the late Arthur Montford. My return from exile coincided with wonderful European nights along the way in the company of my co-commentator Andy Walker, former Motherwell and Celtic player, who not only knew his football well but perhaps even more importantly was no slouch in standing his hand in some odd watering-holes around Europe. He was not slow to speak his mind and of course when you do that you can upset people, as day follows night. I warmed to that assistance though, rather than having a Little Sir Echo beside me. And having a man with authority at your elbow did boost confidence although as I had learned to my cost during the World Cup in France in 1998 you must never make too many assumptions about reputations. For when I was told by *Eurosport* that they had hired the former English captain and Manchester United icon Bryan Robson to be my co-commentator for the Scotland–Norway game I was genuinely excited. We shook hands on the platform in Bordeaux and launched into it. Except I launched, he yawned. He barely opened his mouth. His first response to me was, 'Yes, I agree' and then shut up. Thereafter I suffered acute and repeated embarrassments trying to bring him in only to be met by almost surly indifference for which, as I understand, he was being paid handsomely. It was like he was slumming having to be there to talk about Scotland or even be talking to me in Eurosport. It all added to a deeply disappointing day for me with Scotland only drawing 1–1 with Norway.

But with Andy I was with a soul brother who knew instinctively when and how to fill a gap, thus creating a continuity which I still treasure.

So you can imagine how we felt when the draw was made for the European Cup with Celtic drawn into Group F with the name Manchester United looming above the others, Copenhagen and Benfica. Any association with United and my hackles would go up at the best of times, but augmented now by my own personal rift with Fergie. In the first game at Old Trafford which ended with a 3–2 win for United Nakamura scored with a direct 25-yard free kick which would of itself be worthy plucking from memory lane like a gem in its own right. Except it has shrunk in the wake of the other subsequent event.

Andy and I primed up for the second meeting without any firm view of how it would pan out. I do recall though that in a prominent press conference before he came back over the border Fergie had suggested that he would not send his strongest side out to face Celtic. In fact when the team sheet came out we could see he was to field his strongest 11 of the season fully aware that Celtic had not conceded in their last five Champions League home games. If there was any clue to Celtic's unease anywhere it was in the selection of Bobo Balde for his first competitive start of the season in place of the injured Gary Caldwell. And I mean, against Wayne Rooney? With Ronaldo hovering around there as well? Jings! In fact, after about 20 minutes or so, with United having immeasurably more possession, Celtic's defence harassed though they looked at times were essentially holding out, as I recall. Although mostly backs-to-wall stuff. At half-time I think both Andy and I were emphasising United's overall control looking somewhat ominous for the second half.

Now where was Nakamura? Somewhere in that melting pot but really skirting round the edges. The second half saw a Celtic improvement but not a potentially victorious one with United still creating menace, much the same. So consider what Andy and I are having to contemplate as the game proceeds. United had been principally dominant but with no telling touch of imagination, but at the same time looking as if they will make the break inevitably. Then a free kick is awarded in the 81st minute, Jarosik goes down under a tackle by Vidic. I was slightly surprised. It did not seem wilful. But a free kick nevertheless. I cannot recall the words with Andy at that precise stage, but I swear inwardly we were sharing the same consideration of implausibility. 'Could he really do it again? No! It's just not credible!' That was firmly in the mind. So the man who was about to be subbed paused in front of a smouldering 60,000 and stepped forward with only nine minutes of the tie left. I recall the ball leaving his foot, ascending quickly to clear the wall, then dipping and curving and like threading the needle swept in that minutest space between the outstretched left hand of Van der Sar in goal and the crossbar. And in an instant both Andy and I for the first and probably only time I can recall left our seats in a mix of astonishment and bewilderment as the skies were rent asunder by the eruption of noise from below us. Unforgettable. Celtic 1-0. Yes, the passing of time has made many forget there could have been a colossal anti-climax near the end with the award of a penalty to United but Saha's poor effort was saved by Boruc in goal. The free kick remains a kind of monument in the annals of my broadcasting career because that night it offered me beautifully executed artistry. It hangs in my personal gallery that I visit from time to time still enjoying this special Japanese farewell to Fergie and his men and the general assumption of their impregnability. It reminded me of the days I would sit in a cinema in the east end of Glasgow cheering on Errol Flynn killing Japs and feeling shivers running through me at the sight of even a cinematic yellow face. And now seeing one of those faces scoring a goal like that? It wasn't just a strike. It was a stark reminder that I was ageing and that I could still find it hard to comprehend the changes to my world that were now staring me in the face.

57

The End of the Affair

Rangers v Zenit St Petersburg
0–2
UEFA Cup Final
14 May 2008
Goal: Konstantin Zyryanov

THE CURTAIN DID not come down on my commentating career exactly as I would have planned or would have liked. However, how could I expect to be any different from many others in life who finish the ploughing of their furrows with little fanfare? Except that I had laid great store by one particular evening when the conditions at first seemed set for a public demonstration of Scottish hubris. I was at a European final after all. I should stress there were other commentaries after this one but none which lingered and deposited themselves in the memory like that evening in Manchester. The others afterwards have vanished like they were melted by the incendiary impact of that single night. Yes, Rangers playing in a European final against a Russian side, cloaked in the kind of anonymity as all these sides seemed to be from that part of the continent, was finality for me in the commentating role. In keeping with the other European finals I had attended I knew I would have to constrain my appetite for a Scottish victory and not treat the Russians like hostiles.

Of course, this final was unfailingly intriguing, for here were two managers opposing each other but whom I regarded almost as blood brothers. Dick Advocaat in charge of Zenit, had won the domestic treble for Ibrox in his very first season in Scotland in 1998 as Rangers manager, and in the following year won the league title by a record 21 points margin. Of course he had a different accent from the man he had replaced, Walter Smith, but for me they seemed to speak the same football language. They were both coherent. I could understand what they were talking about which was not always the case in managerial settings. And from both of them I learned a lot about the pressures they faced as they both allowed me entry to some of their intimate thoughts about the Scottish scene. And now, Walter back at Ibrox, with renewed self-confidence, and Advocaat still fending off criticism of his spending sprees which many linked to Rangers' growing financial problems, they were opposed to each other, like relatives about to enter a dispute about the last will and testament of their common benefactor.

I sat nursing an initial problem with this game. I was choked by the vivid memories of the other European finals I had attended. Firstly, there had been Lisbon in 1967. There I had been the headmaster of a school released from work for three days simply to add commentary for the occasion. And there under the blue skies and the scathing sun watched Celtic stun the continent with an audacity that fitted the climate perfectly. Then in 1972 in the vast Nou Camp in Barcelona watched Rangers triumph over Moscow Dynamo with the addition of spectator involvement that took place in the velvety atmosphere of a perfect Spanish evening. And 11 years later in the northern city of Gothenburg watched Aberdeen cope with the sleety atmosphere of Sweden and leave the Spaniards floundering. These had all been triumphs and indeed in all three of these finals at no stage did I ever feel any imminent sense of loss. I carried all that with me to Manchester on that early summer day but was struck by an entirely different atmosphere. There was nothing in that city that provided a sense of special theatre for a cup final. And even before a ball was kicked I was finding it difficult to see Rangers as potential winners, for reasons that were difficult to clarify in the mind. It was weighing me down.

In the first instance we learned on arrival that the streets of that city were awash with the problems of how ticketless supporters were trying to cope with frustration and disappointment of being unable to follow the action. It is the only time I sat in a commentary position trying also to keep pace with the developments in the streets outside, as news began to filter through to the commentary position that an invasion of something like 200,000 Rangers supporters had encountered difficulties particularly with the failure of a giant television screen set up publicly in the acreage of Piccadilly in the centre of the city. I simply could not get out of my mind the thought of scores of supporters from the north unable to see or hear anything of the match. So essentially this was a cup final of annoyance, discomfort and, as a commentator, realising that if what we were hearing from the streets was accurate, that the whole occasion would be assessed and judged completely differently from the other four other European finals in Lisbon, Milan, Barcelona and Gothenburg. I wrestled with a game that was bleak by comparison with these other climaxes. From the very outset I knew this would offer a different experience in the City of Manchester Stadium.

As for the game itself, there was never any likelihood of Rangers changing their style for this match. Throughout the competition they had based their method on patience and endurance and given that they were also favourites to pick up a domestic treble their manager Walter Smith was in no frame of mind to please the purists who think differently about how finals should be approached. He knew of course that the Zenit manager Dick Advocaat had shown great capacity for counterattacking and had run up high-scores against Bayern Munich and Bayer Leverkusen. This intensified Smith's cautious approach. I couldn't fend off the feeling that with the problems we were hearing out on the streets that this was the most challenging of all the finals I had encountered. And then I found myself coming to the conclusion that Rangers were not going to win this game. That thought embedded itself in the mind just after half-time. And curiously it was at a spell when Rangers looked to be asserting themselves better and claiming more possession. But I could not cast off the feeling that they were to be losers. That thought would not budge. I tried to dress it up in some more encouraging descriptions of their attacks. The Rangers captain Barry Ferguson, for example, looked to be tripped by the Zenit goalkeeper Malafeev in a melee in the box and I made much of Rangers' penalty claim, completely ignored by the referee Fröjdfeldt. All it did was intensify my feeling that Rangers were doomed.

But there was one player who stood out amongst the drabness. Andrey Arshavin. I had watched him string England along in Moscow when he had been a stand-out in their recent victory over them for Russia. That same slickness and apparent ease of control was perhaps not as prominent, but it was there in bursts. And, indeed, on the half-time whistle the referee failed to see Kirk Broadfoot use his arm to block an Arshavin cross with the Russian players fulminating as a result.

During the interval we learned more about the reaction in the streets.

There had been trouble and arrests made which given the failure of the giant screen in the city hardly surprised us. I mentioned this in commentary passingly, so as not to totally ignore what would certainly be a major issue to be addressed whatever the outcome of the game. But the balance of play I was describing did not lessen my feeling that Rangers were vulnerable. I tried to enthuse about them but felt myself becoming slightly theatrical. Zenit were solid if largely unenterprising as the second half wore on. But when the opening goal came I did feel the pain of the commentary words themselves which was to describe a move that was hardly of stunning originality but of effective orthodoxy. It was in the 72nd minute. Arshavin, unsurprisingly, split the Rangers defence with an incisive pass through the middle. A ball that actually passed through Cuellar's legs for Denisov to run on to. He took only one touch before sending it past the Rangers goalkeeper Neil Alexander. 1–0.

It's what I had expected and of all the four finals I had experienced with the Scottish sides it was the first time I had felt the absolute certainty of defeat that I would have to summarise, and mentally I had begun to prepare for it. That is why I recall the final goal so vividly by Zyryanov. It typified the night. With an element of slick one-touch passing Konstantin Zyryanov was left with only a slight touch from about 18 inches to score the second. A kind of school-playground goal for a European final. I look back on describing that last goal with the realisation I was uttering a kind of epitaph on the Scottish game. For, as never before, I was aware of speaking to a divided audience. Since the earliest days I had lived with and worked in the fractured nature of the football that is innocuously defined as the Old Firm. At that moment in Manchester as defeat was confirmed I knew there would be different responses among the television audience, gloom and anger, contrasting with the purring contentment of those of the other faith. An anonymous Russian had scored a goal that painfully reminded me of that.

After the presentation of the cup to the Russian side we were to learn that the Manchester city authorities were describing the events of the evening in the streets as if it were a reminder of the blitz during the war. It made the final itself seem now like some innocuous sideshow we had been covering. At the same time I felt like I had buried a career there in Manchester. Anything after that was to pale by comparison and would seem of little consequence. But I also relate to that feeling of finality with the deep satisfaction of recalling the days when I felt I was sharing emotions with an entire nation whenever I ushered a goal into the public domain, free of Orwellian VAR. And often it made me feel like I was back to bulging Hampden Park in 1946 when in short-pants and crouched against the retaining wall at the foot of the terracing I watched Jimmy Delaney score that last minute winner against the English, that to a post-war kid was like having all the wrongs of the world put to right in a single act. And, of learning dramatically, that very day, of how the word 'Goal' could mean so much, to so many.

Acknowledgements

I STILL OWE a lot to my researcher Pat Woods who has stuck by my elbow throughout all of my books and was an invaluable help again. I am grateful to my former co-commentator Andy Walker for his important recollections of many of the incidents described in the book. That excellent broadcaster Bernard Ponsonby, of many years with Scottish Television, assisted me through certain passages for clarification. I had specific technical computer problems which were solved for me by Mrs Fiona Miller and without whom there would have been no progress. Invaluable were the interviews in the past I had with some of Scotland's greatest players, John Greig, Billy McNeill, Danny McGrain, Sandy Jardine, Ally McCoist, Charlie Nicholas and of course some of the great managers, Jock Stein, Walter Smith, Alex Ferguson just to mention a few of the many. They provided a composite picture of great days for the Scottish game that I was fortunate to help bring to a nationwide audience.

Luath Press Limited

committed to publishing well written books worth reading

LUATH PRESS takes its name from Robert Burns, whose little collie Luath (*Gael.*, swift or nimble) tripped up Jean Armour at a wedding and gave him the chance to speak to the woman who was to be his wife and the abiding love of his life. Burns called one of the 'Twa Dogs' Luath after Cuchullin's hunting dog in Ossian's *Fingal*. Luath Press was established in 1981 in the heart of Burns country, and is now based a few steps up the road from Burns' first lodgings on Edinburgh's Royal Mile. Luath offers you distinctive writing with a hint of unexpected pleasures.

Most bookshops in the UK, the US, Canada, Australia, New Zealand and parts of Europe, either carry our books in stock or can order them for you. To order direct from us, please send a £sterling cheque, postal order, international money order or your credit card details (number, address of cardholder and expiry date) to us at the address below. Please add post and packing as follows: UK – £1.00 per delivery address; overseas surface mail – £2.50 per delivery address; overseas airmail – £3.50 for the first book to each delivery address, plus £1.00 for each additional book by airmail to the same address. If your order is a gift, we will happily enclose your card or message at no extra charge.

Luath Press Limited
543/2 Castlehill
The Royal Mile
Edinburgh EH1 2ND
Scotland
Telephone: 0131 225 4326 (24 hours)
Email: sales@luath.co.uk
Website: www.luath.co.uk